CULT...
South Africa

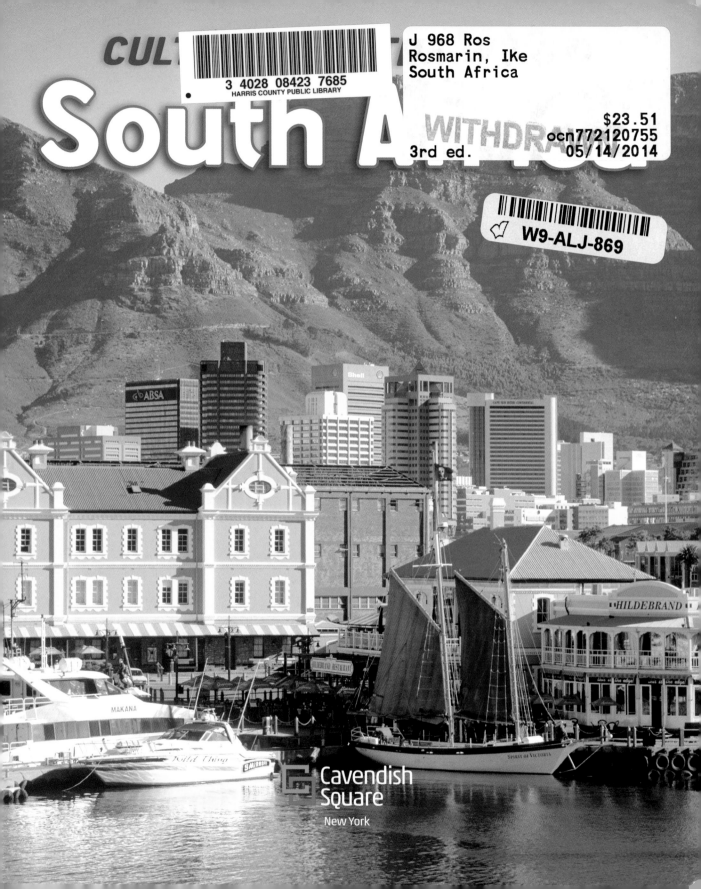

Cavendish
Square
New York

Published in 2014 by Cavendish Square Publishing, LLC
303 Park Avenue South, Suite 1247, New York, NY 10010

Third Edition

This publication is published with arrangement with Marshall Cavendish International (Asia) Pte Ltd.

Copyright © 2014 Marshall Cavendish International (Asia) Pte Ltd.

Website: cavendishsq.com

Cultures of the World is a registered trademark of Times Publishing Limited.

This publication represents the opinions and views of the author based on his or her personal experience, knowledge, and research. The information in this book serves as a general guide only. The author and publisher have used their best efforts in preparing this book and disclaim liability rising directly or indirectly from the use and application of this book.

CPSIA Compliance Information: Batch #WW14CSQ

All websites were available and accurate when this book was sent to press.

Library of Congress Cataloging-in-Publication Data
Rosmarin, Ike.
South Africa / by Ike Rosmarin, Dee Rissik and Josie Elias.
   p. cm. — (Cultures of the world)
Includes index.
ISBN 978-0-76148-015-0 (hardcover) ISBN 978-1-62712-626-7 (paperback) ISBN 978-0-76148-023-5 (ebook)
1. South Africa — Juvenile literature. I. Rosmarin, Ike, 1915-. II. Title.
DT1719 .R67 2014
968—d23

Writers: Ike Rosmarin, Dee Rissik and Josie Elias
Editor: Mindy Pang
Designer: Benson Tan

PICTURE CREDITS
Cover: © Richard I'Anson / Getty Images
Corbis / Click Photos: 56, 112, 128 • Inmagine.com: 1, 3, 5, 6, 7, 8, 9, 10, 11, 12, 13, 14, 15, 18, 19, 20, 22, 24, 25, 26, 30, 33, 34, 35, 38, 40, 41, 42, 45, 47, 50, 52, 53, 54, 55, 57, 58, 60, 62, 63, 64, 65, 66, 67, 68, 69, 70, 72, 73, 74, 75, 76, 77, 79, 80, 81, 82, 83, 84, 85, 86, 88, 90, 91, 92, 94, 96, 98, 99, 101, 104, 105, 106, 107, 108, 109, 110, 111, 114, 115, 116, 117, 118, 119, 120, 121, 122, 124, 125, 126, 127, 129, 130, 131

PRECEDING PAGE
The Victoria and Alfred Waterfront in the heart of Cape Town's harbor.

Printed in the United States of America

CONTENTS

SOUTH AFRICA TODAY

SOUTH AFRICA HAS A COLORFUL AND DRAMATIC HISTORY, NOT only clouded at times by racial conflict and oppression but also filled with the goodwill of millions of individuals from a wide mix of cultures and beliefs. This has been woven into a unique tapestry that now makes up the Rainbow Nation, as it was named by Nelson Mandela, South Africa's first true president.

The new country, born in 1994 after its first-ever democratic elections, has taken its seat at the global table. Having been cut off from most of the world for many years due to apartheid—a policy of racial discrimination by a white minority government over a black majority—the country is now moving ahead under a new government. The combination of democracy and favorable economic stability has created new opportunities and new challenges.

Approximately 53 million people live in South Africa: whites, blacks, Coloreds, and Asians. About 79 percent of the population is black, 9 percent is white, 9 percent is Colored, and 2.5 percent is Asian. There are 11 official languages. Although English is the mother tongue of only 8.2 percent of the population, it is the language most widely understood and the second language of the majority of South Africans.

Rows of houses in Soweto, named "matchbox" houses by the locals due to their size and basic design. These four-room establishments were occupied by the first black migrants to the city.

According to the constitution everyone has the right to freedom of religion, thought, and opinion. Almost 80 percent of the population follows the Christian faith. The largest group of Christian churches is the African independent churches (AICs) that are represented by the Zionist or Apostolic churches. Other major religious groups are Muslims, Hindus, and Jews.

There is a big discrepancy in the standard of housing in South Africa. In the cities and more affluent areas people live in houses or apartments that have all the amenities usually taken for granted—running water, electricity, and waste disposal. But in mid-2009 it was estimated that there are still approximately 2,700 informal settlements across the country, accommodating more than 1.2 million households. Many of these settlements are overcrowded, unhygienic, and do not have running water or electricity. In the sprawling townships of Soweto, Alexandra, and Orange Farm some of the houses do have running water, but the occupants are unable to pay the utility bills and the supply gets cut off. To help address this problem the Department of Human Settlements was given the mandate to transform the country's residential areas. Between 1994 and 2010 the government built 2.7 million homes for South Africans, providing accommodation to more than 13 million people. Different types of housing were built, from single units to double-story units and rows of attached houses, with the aim of eradicating the informal settlements as quickly as possible. This program is ongoing and the government has recognized that it is also essential to create jobs and employment to raise the standard of living and income of this sector of the population.

The Expanded Public Works Programme (EPWP) aims to create employment opportunities to alleviate poverty and unemployment through the creation of labor-intensive work opportunities. The EPWP's mandate includes caring for the elderly and sick, educating preschool children, cleaning up the environment, as well as upgrading and maintaining crucial infrastructure such as roads, bridges, water, and sanitation.

Ranked by the United Nations Conference on Trade and Development (UNCTAD) as among the Emerging 7 (E7) group of nations South Africa has one of the strongest economies in Africa. There has been an increase of income across all groups and the economy is continuing to grow. South Africa is committed to the New Partnership for Africa's Development (NEPAD). The continent is an important trade partner for South Africa, and South Africa is the single largest source of foreign investment in Africa.

South Africa is a beautiful country boasting a variety of activities and attractions. The people are culturally diverse and their lifestyles change according to their income and preferences. The cities are vibrant with restaurants, shopping malls, cinema complexes, and shops. Restaurants offer a variety of exotic and traditional cuisine, using fresh, homegrown ingredients. People enjoy eating out and socializing either with family or friends. Barbecues are also very popular. There are many natural attractions, theme parks, and game parks.

The Coronation Double Century Cycle Challenge is a yearly event that attracts dedicated cyclists from all over the country. The course travels through picturesque areas such as the Tradouw Pass.

South Africans generally enjoy an active outdoor lifestyle, as the climate is good. People living near the coast go to the beach to enjoy the surf and sand—usually under the watchful eye of a qualified lifeguard—and they swim within the area defined by shark safety nets. South Africa is one of the few countries in the world that provides the opportunity for cage fishing and shark encounters. It also offers cage diving in several locations along the Western Cape shoreline, including Cape Town. Sports are played at all levels, from amateur to club, national, and international levels. Cycling, quad-biking, swimming, surfing, jogging, running, hiking, horseback riding, sand boarding, kite surfing, paragliding, snow-skiing, and abseiling are all popular and available.

Tourists on a safari ride take a close look at some giraffes in the Glen Afric reserve, located in the Gauteng province.

Walking safaris offer a unique way to explore the African bush, and are popular with all age groups. Safaris in four-wheel-drive vehicles are also favored, providing the opportunity to encounter some of South Africa's famous wildlife in its natural environment. The world-renowned Kruger National Park was established in 1898 to protect the wildlife of the South African Lowveld. Kruger is home to an impressive number of bird, animal, and plant species. The park is best known for its large expanses of wilderness and big game sightings, but archaeological sites and bushman rock paintings are also located here and are conserved along with the park's natural assets. The South African National Parks (SANParks) employs environmental crime investigators and rangers in a bid to protect the animals from poachers. In the first three months of 2012, 130 rhino carcasses were found discarded by poachers after the rhinos had been dehorned and killed. A total of 31 suspected poachers were arrested in the same period.

In 2010 South Africa hosted the World Cup football tournament. This event accelerated government expenditure on transportation, transportation links, and infrastructure, and was very significant in a country that was for many years banned from most international sporting events because of its apartheid policy. For South Africa hosting the tournament was an intrinsic part of building a nation that is nonracist and living by the concepts of equality and human solidarity. The investment in the World Cup football tournament included building a stadium and all the associated requirements of a world-class event—sports, recreation, arts, and culture programs were initiated, volunteers were trained, marketing and advertising campaigns were established, safety and security measures improved, and emergency and medical services were expanded.

South Africa is facing a significant challenge in creating a better life for all of its people. To tackle the issue of unemployment, the government has invested heavily in education, aiming to create more jobs for a more skilled workforce. The unemployment rate in South Africa was estimated at 25.6 percent in the second quarter of 2013. Unemployment is highest among people aged 15 to 34 years. The unemployment rate for women is higher than the national average and people without a matriculation certificate account for the highest number of unemployed. The Bill of Rights contained in the constitution stipulates that everyone has the right to a basic education, including adult education. The largest proportion of the country's budget is spent on education. In 2012 a total of 98 percent of children aged 7 to 15 years were enrolled in schools. Vulnerable South Africans may apply for social grants to help with schooling and other expenses, and are also eligible for tax relief if they are low earners.

Children queuing to enter their reading class in Cape Town.

South Africa has the highest incidence of people living with human immunodeficiency virus (HIV) and acquired immunodeficiency syndrome (AIDS) in the world. It is estimated that 5.6 million people are infected in South Africa. Approximately 300,000 people die of AIDS-related causes every year; that is almost 1,000 people a day. HIV prevalence in children over the age of two is more pronounced in KwaZulu-Natal (15.8 percent) than in the Western Cape (3.8 percent). An estimated 63,000 children were infected with HIV in 2011, reflecting poor prevention of mother-to-child transmission. To combat the problem of AIDS and HIV, the government launched a major HIV testing and counseling campaign in 2010, and has also made antiretroviral (ARV) treatment free to pregnant HIV-positive women. Communication campaigns have been established to raise awareness about HIV and AIDS, including publicizing the availability of free testing and counseling in health clinics.

South Africa has embarked on a set of initiatives aimed at accelerating development and growth that will assist the entire population. Its aim is to defeat poverty and the negative legacy of apartheid and to promote democracy, peace, prosperity, and social progress. New policies are being made to enable all citizens to share in the wealth of one of the most blessed countries on the African continent. With its abundant natural beauty, its mineral and agricultural wealth, and its drive to right past wrongs, South Africa looks set for a promising future.

GEOGRAPHY

An aerial view of Cape Town.

SOUTH AFRICA IS LOCATED at the southern tip of the African continent. It is bordered by Mozambique and Swaziland to the northeast, Zimbabwe and Botswana to the north, and Namibia to the northwest. The southeastern region of the country surrounds Lesotho.

South Africa lies between two oceans: the Indian in the east and the Atlantic in the west. These two oceans meet at the southernmost tip of the country and of the continent, Cape Agulhas.

The Cape Agulhas Lighthouse, located near the coastal village of L'Agulhas. It was the third lighthouse built in South Africa and has guided the navigation of plenty of ships in the area.

Occupying the southernmost area of the continent of Africa, South Africa has a long coastline that stretches more than 1,553 miles (2,500 kilometers) from the subtropical border with Mozambique on the Indian Ocean coast southward around the tip of Africa and then north to the desert border with Namibia on the Atlantic coast.

A wide landscape with rock plateaus at the Royal Natal National Park. The main attraction of the park is the Amphitheatre, a rock wall about five kilometers in length. It is also the location of Tugela Falls, the world's second highest waterfall.

South Africa has a variety of geographic regions, including mountains, deserts, plateaus, forests, beaches, and rivers. Its position at the tip of Africa and at the junction of the Indian and Atlantic oceans makes it important in world trade.

LANDSCAPE

South Africa covers a total area of 470,693 square miles (1,219,090 square km), nearly three times the size of California. There are four main regions: the veld, which refers to open country with grassy patches that is used for pasturage and farmland; the desert areas; the Great Escarpment and highlands; and the coastal region.

Together the desert areas and the veld form a large plateau in a semicircular shape that occupies the country's interior. The coastal region is a narrow strip fringing the plateau on three sides. Forming a mountainous barrier between the plateau and the coast is the Great Escarpment. It is made up of several mountain ranges that shape itself into a rocky wall along the eastern and southern edges of the plateau. The Great Escarpment starts near Zimbabwe in the north, and toward the south the Drakensberg range becomes higher and more dramatic. One of South Africa's highest mountains, Champagne Castle, is found in the Central Drakensberg range and reaches a height of 11,079 feet (3,377 meters).

The wall then swings west, curving across the southern part of the country in a series of smaller mountain ranges. In this southwestern area of the country it forms two extensive plateaus: the Great Karoo and the Little Karoo, which lie just north of the mountains. These plateaus are semi-desert regions, but crops are grown and sheep are raised in fertile areas that receive enough rain during seasonal downpours.

In the east rocky foothills of the Great Escarpment divide the central plateau from the low-lying subtropical region in the Mpumalanga province. A narrow coastal strip of smaller mountains and hills of between about 700 and 1,600 feet (213 and 488 m) above sea level runs along much of the coastline.

Land in the northwest of the country receives very little rainfall and is covered by desert and semi-desert. This area borders the Kalahari Desert, which extends over northern South Africa, Botswana, and Namibia.

Table Mountain, overlooking Cape Town, has a flat-topped silhouette that makes it a popular destination for tourists, be it hiking or sightseeing. The clouds over the mountain form what is commonly called the 'Table Cloth'.

Red dunes of the semi-arid Kalahari Desert in the Kgalagadi transfrontier park of North Cape in South Africa.

CLIMATE

South Africa suffers from inconsistent rainfall and is often plagued by droughts. It is a relatively dry country, with an average rainfall of about 18.3 inches (464 mm) compared with the world average rainfall of about 33.9 inches (860 mm). Only one-third of the land receives the minimum annual rainfall needed to raise crops. The eastern half of the country is wetter, while much of the west is suitable only for grazing.

In South Africa the climate varies across the country. In the east summer temperatures average around 75°F (24°C), with daytime highs of 100°F (38°C). The Central area sees average summer temperatures of 66°F (19°C), and daytime highs of 80°F (27°C). Ocean breezes bring the average temperature down to 68°F (20°C) on the southeastern and southern coast, but daytime highs stay in the mid-70s (24°C).

In the winter average temperatures drop to a third of summer's, especially in the higher central areas, but this seldom falls below freezing. In the high regions of the Drakensberg Mountains it is much colder. Snow falls and usually settles for a few weeks almost every winter.

Much of South Africa is located just below the Tropic of Capricorn so the country experiences warm temperatures and a great deal of sunshine. Because South Africa is in the Southern Hemisphere winter (May—July) is the sunniest and driest time of the year. The Western Cape is the exception and gets most of its rain at this time of the year.

RIVERS AND LAKES

There are three major rivers in South Africa. The Orange River, the most extensive waterway, is about 1,300 miles (2,092 km) long and flows from the Lesotho Highlands to the Atlantic Ocean at Alexander Bay. It provides irrigation to the Northern Cape as well as hydroelectricity to other parts of the country.

The Vaal River, 750 miles (1,207 km) long, flows southwest from Sterkfontein Beacon near Breyten in eastern Mpumalanga province, and forms part of the border between this province and Free State. The Vaal eventually joins the Orange River near Douglas in the Northern Cape.

The Limpopo River rises as the Krokodil (Crocodile) River in the Witwatersrand near Johannesburg. It is 1,100 miles (1,770 km) long and flows north, then northeast, forming South Africa's border with Zimbabwe. It then cuts through Mozambique and empties into the Indian Ocean.

South Africa's erratic weather causes many small rivers to run dry for long periods. There are few freshwater lakes, but man-made dams have helped to increase water resources for consumption and agriculture. Some marshlands, such as Lake Saint Lucia in KwaZulu-Natal, form during the rainy season.

The Orange River was named by Colonel Robert Gordon, commander of the Dutch East India Company garrison, in honor of Prince William V of the Royal Dutch House of Orange, and not because the color of the river's water is orange, as popularly believed.

WATER

Water is a critical resource for South Africa. There is a limited and irregular supply of freshwater through rainfall. Less than 10 percent of rainfall in South Africa is available as surface water. This is one of the lowest conversion rations worldwide. Groundwater resources in the country are also limited.

River water is regulated but in many areas demand still does not meet supply, and the quality is below standard and not potable. The growing needs of an increasing population for both domestic and agricultural use have placed heavy demand on this valuable resource.

Growing demand is partly responsible for the short supply of freshwater but loss of natural habitat and possibly climate change are also issues. South Africa has been heavily settled for many centuries and as a result large swathes of natural vegetation have been cleared for urban development and agriculture.

FAUNA AND FLORA

Because of the abundance and variety of plant and animal life, South Africa boasts one of the most diverse wildlife displays on Earth. In spite of the wasteful and often needless overkill of game in the 19th and 20th centuries, much of the wildlife has survived. The establishment of the Kruger National Park in 1898 marked the turning point of game conservation across the country.

An elephant herd walks to the water hole in the Addo Elephant National Park. The park was formed to save 11 elephants on the brink of extinction. It eventually became a great conservation success, with more than 350 currently residing here.

NATIONAL PARKS

Established in 1926, the leading conservation authority in South Africa is SANParks. SANParks is responsible for 14,483 square miles (37,510 square km) of protected land in 21 national parks across South Africa. The most famous of these is the Kruger National Park, which supports the widest variety of wildlife species on the African continent. The Kruger National Park has an area of more than 7,800 square miles (about 20,201 square km). Numerous roads as well as more than 30 rest camps and lodges with beds, shops, and restaurants have been built within the park to accommodate thousands of visitors. But it is so large that the animals remain undisturbed. It is one of the few places left in the world where one can observe life in the wild as it must have been thousands of years ago.

The country has a very wide variety of game species, including elephants, giraffes, zebras, lions, leopards, cheetahs, hyenas, polecats, badgers, jackals, baboons, monkeys, antelopes, crocodiles, and snakes. Conservation has meant that South Africa still has large herds of elephants as well as good numbers of white rhinoceros and hippopotamus among the many hundreds of other wild animal species.

Ten percent of the planet's known species of birds, including the ostrich and the strictly terrestrial kori bustard (*Ardeotis kori kori*), which can weigh up to 40 pounds (18 kilograms), are found here. In the game parks, animals still roam freely in their natural habitat.

The varied climate and lack of rainfall determine much of South Africa's flora. Where rainfall is light, vegetation is poor, and only dry scrub survives. Where rainfall is heavy, palm trees and forests of yellowwood (*Podocarpus latifolius*), black ironwood (*Olea capensis* subsp. *macrocarpa*), black stinkwood (*Ocotea bullata*), and Clanwilliam cedar (*Widdringtonia cedarbergensis*) grow.

Western Cape province has a remarkable collection of spectacular indigenous flowers and shrubs called *fynbos* (f-AY-n-BAWS), Afrikaans for "fine-leaved plants." The province has 8,500 species and accounts for more than a third of the country's floral kingdom. The national flower, the king protea (*Protea cynaroides*), can be found in this province.

Since much of South Africa is grassland, it is not surprising that about 500 species of grass are found in the country.

The major cities have a number of botanical gardens. The most famous is the Kirstenbosch National Botanical Garden that lies on the eastern slopes of Table Mountain in the Cape Town suburbs. More than 4,700 of the estimated 20,000 species of indigenous South African flora are featured there. The botanical gardens in Durban have a wide variety of tropical plants because of the hot, humid climate.

REGIONS

After its first democratic elections in 1994, South Africa was divided into nine provinces of varying sizes and population densities. They are:

WESTERN CAPE A Mediterranean climate makes this province suitable for growing crops, especially deciduous fruit and wine grapes. Cape Agulhas, the southernmost tip of Africa, is located in this province. Cape Town is the legislative capital of South Africa.

Namaqualand daisies, or *Dimorphotheca sinuata*, bloom in the Northern Cape in early spring. Other than yellow, the flowers also take on an orange or white color.

NORTHERN CAPE Known as diamond country, this is one of the largest provinces but the least populated, as most of it is semi-desert. Areas along the Orange River and in the southern sections are fertile and good farming land where cotton, dates, and grapes are grown.

NORTH WEST This province has fertile soil for growing crops, especially corn. Cattle are also raised here.

EASTERN CAPE The coast in this region offers some of the most beautiful scenery and pristine beaches in the country. Port Elizabeth on the shores of Algoa Bay is the capital of the Eastern Cape. Inland it is a good cattle- and sheep-raising area.

A mixed cattle herd on a field in the small village of Fouriesburg in Free State.

KWAZULU-NATAL The lush subtropical climate in this region is ideal for growing sugarcane. Cattle graze on the lush farmlands. The province has the country's largest Zulu population.

FREE STATE Although areas of this province are fairly dry, it is good farming land and has large cornfields. The northern area has fertile soil and good rainfall, creating excellent conditions for wheat, sunflowers, cattle, and game farming. Fields of corn and sunflowers are grown in the central area, which also has some of the country's most productive gold mines. Bloemfontein, South Africa's judicial capital, is located in this province.

GAUTENG Although it is the smallest, this province is the country's economic hub. Johannesburg, the largest city in South Africa, is located here. The city of Pretoria is one of the country's three capital cities and is officially the executive or administrative capital.

MPUMALANGA The fertile lands near the Great Escarpment yield nuts, citrus fruit, coffee, and timber. The region's greatest attraction is the Kruger National Park.

The cityscape of Port Elizabeth.

LIMPOPO This province has many provincial and private game reserves, subtropical fruit farms, and game ranches. It shares international borders with three other African countries: Botswana, Zimbabwe, and Mozambique.

CITIES

South Africa's cities are comparatively young. Modern and well planned, they are home to more than half of South Africa's population.

CAPE TOWN This coastal town nestled next to Table Mountain in the Western Cape has a population of 3.74 million people. It is the republic's legislative center and an important seaport sited at the meeting point of major sea routes.

PRETORIA With a population of 2.34 million, South Africa's administrative capital has hilltop government buildings overlooking most of the city.

JOHANNESBURG Just 28 miles (45 km) south of Pretoria is South Africa's most populous city. Johannesburg is the provincial capital of Gauteng and has a population of 3.8 million in its metropolitan area. With its large surrounding townships, such as Soweto and others on the eastern side of the city, its overall population is probably closer to 10 million. This vibrant, modern city was founded in 1886 on some of the richest gold deposits in the world. It is often called E'goli, an African nickname that refers both to the gold mining that led to its founding and its current status as the country's business and economic center.

DURBAN This is the country's second-largest city, with a population of 3.7 million. It is located in the Eastern Cape and is the largest port in South Africa and the African continent. As such it has developed into a major regional transportation center. Similar to all South Africa's major cities, Durban's population is diverse, with a large Indian sector. Because of its subtropical climate and long sandy beaches, it is also an important holiday resort.

PORT ELIZABETH This port city is situated on Algoa Bay and has a population of about 1.5 million, making it the fifth-largest city in South Africa in terms of population. It was founded in 1820 when the first British settlers arrived by ship. Today it is an industrial hub with large automobile manufacturing factories. The main harbor has a container terminal, a fruit terminal, and a manganese terminal.

INTERNET LINKS

www.centralkaroo.co.za/

This site contains detailed information on the Great Karoo in the Western Cape, one of the world's most unique arid zones.

www.zulu.org.za/

This is the official website of the KwaZulu-Natal tourism authority, with links to a variety of topics and many photos.

www.port-elizabeth.org.za/

This website contains information on Port Elizabeth, including the history, museums, townships, nature reserves, and attractions.

HISTORY

The Voortrekker Monument was inaugurated in 1949 to pay homage to the pioneer Voortrekkers who embarked on the Great Trek, a migration from British control of the Cape colony, from 1835 to 1854.

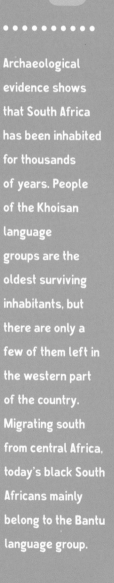

MANY ARCHAEOLOGISTS BELIEVE that the prehistoric ancestors of human beings lived in the Sterkfontein caves, about 30 miles (48.3 km) from where Johannesburg is now. The skeletons of these prehistoric ancestors belong to the species *Australopithecus africanus* and were discovered in 1947.

The remains of the apelike beings found here are 4 million years old and provide clues about the first human inhabitants of South Africa. One of the earliest known peoples was the San, or Bushmen, who were hunter-gatherers. Many intermarried or settled in communities, but a number remained nomadic hunters in the semi-desert regions of Northern Cape. (They also live in Botswana and Namibia.) Other early immigrants to the southern part of the country included the pastoral Khoikhoi herders who bred cattle, sheep, and goats.

THE SOUTHERN AFRICAN IRON AGE

The Iron Age inhabitants of South Africa in the 11th and 12th centuries were the ancestors of the black South Africans of today.

The first black immigrants to South Africa were the Sotho, Nguni, Tsonga, and Venda from central Africa. By the 14th century the Nguni occupied large areas in KwaZulu-Natal and Eastern Cape. Groups of Sotho spread to the southwest and occupied parts of what is now northwestern Limpopo, while smaller groups of Tsonga and Venda moved into Limpopo province. These groups formed kingdoms and lived by herding and farming.

Archaeological evidence shows that South Africa has been inhabited for thousands of years. People of the Khoisan language groups are the oldest surviving inhabitants, but there are only a few of them left in the western part of the country. Migrating south from central Africa, today's black South Africans mainly belong to the Bantu language group.

The rebellious Boers battled against the ruling British in the First Boer War. The British were defeated and an armistice was agreed upon.

Clashes occurred in a fight for dominance of the land, causing division within the various kingdoms. Even though there has been extensive cross-cultural mixing among all the races, many of these ethnic divisions still exist today.

COLONISTS

In 1488 the Europeans arrived. A Portuguese mariner, Bartolomeu Dias, was the first to circumnavigate the Cape, naming it Cabo de Boa Esperanca, or the Cape of Good Hope. Ten years later Vasco da Gama, another Portuguese, passed the Cape en route to India. In November 1497 the Portuguese set foot on South African soil for the first time at present-day Saint Helena Bay on the west coast and encountered the first Khoi-Khoi. In 1498 da Gama reached the mouth of the Limpopo River and from there sailed across to India via the Cape of Malabar, thereby establishing the monopoly of the Portuguese sea route to India.

In 1602 the Vereenigde Landsche Ge-Oktroyeerde Oost-Indische Compagnie (VOC) trading company received a charter from the States General, the highest authority in the Republic of the United Netherlands, entailing a trading monopoly and the right to acquire and govern Dutch possessions in the Orient for 21 years. This was extended in 1623 and 1647.

In 1647 the Dutch ship *Nieuwe Haerlem* was wrecked in Table Bay. Leendert Janszen was instructed to remain there with some crew to look after the cargo. On his return to Holland he was told to write a feasibility report on the establishment of a refreshment station at the Cape. In 1651 the Dutch East India Company sent Jan van Riebeeck to establish a settlement at the Cape. Jan van Riebeeck arrived in Table Bay in 1652 and chose the site on which to build a fort and a refreshment station to provide fresh water, fruit, vegetables, and meat for passing Dutch fleets en route to India. He was also instructed to build a hospital for ill sailors.

In the late 1650s African, Indian, and Southeast Asian slaves were brought to the colony. In 1655 the first corn seeds and grape vines were introduced to the Cape from Holland. With imported slave labor the colony prospered. There were good harvests of corn and grapes were grown for wine production. The first of the company servants were freed and given permission to farm and keep livestock on freehold land along the Liesbeeck River. These ex-servants were called free burghers. They were exempt from taxation and given access to slaves. More settlers moved inland and started farming the fertile soil.

A painting of Jan van Riebeeck's landing at Table Bay. His arrival marked the beginning of white settlement in the region.

Throughout this period there were disagreements and skirmishes over the ownership of the land between the Dutch and the Khoi-Khoi. There were also thefts of Dutch possessions. In 1657 watch houses and fortifications were incorporated in to the settlements to keep out the thieves. This was the first introduction of the official policy of territorial segregation in South Africa. In 1659 the First Khoi-Khoi—Dutch War broke out with a series of armed confrontations over the ownership of land.

In 1688 about 150 French Huguenot refugees arrived and settled mainly in Franschhoek. By 1779 the white population had grown to approximately 15,000.

INTO THE INTERIOR

In the 1690s trek Boers (BOO-ers), semi-nomadic Dutch farmers and cattle grazers who wanted to move beyond the official borders of the Cape and out of reach of the authority of the Company, advanced into the interior. They encountered black indigenous peoples who had been emigrating southward. The various black indigenous groups were divided into kingdoms, each headed by a chief. A chief's wealth was measured by how many farms, people, and herds of cattle he controlled. The trek Boers were forbidden to raid the livestock of the Khoi-Khoi or to drive them off the land, but some of them did so even though they were punished by the Company if discovered. The San and Khoi-Khoi retaliated by attacking, burning, and raiding farms.

Boers surrounded at the Brandwater Basin of the Orange Free State during the Anglo-Boer War. The Orange Free State, an independent Boer republic, was formally annexed as Orange River Colony in 1900.

In 1820 some 5,000 immigrants arrived from Britain and were sent to farm in Eastern Cape. The British wanted to increase their influence in the Cape and provide a buffer zone against the Xhosas (KAW-sahs) who were establishing themselves there. When the British started encroaching on Xhosa land, fierce fighting between the two groups broke out.

Many Boers in Eastern Cape felt that they were not being represented by the British and saw no future under British rule. In 1836 Dutch families began crossing the Orange River into the interior. The breakaway farmers were known as Voortrekkers (FOO-ehr-trekkers). The trek Boer of the 1690s was not the same as a Voortrekker. Voortrekkers left the Cape Colony in the 1830s in a series of treks, intending to settle permanently in areas of the interior that were not under British rule. Over the next decade an estimated 15,000 men, women, and children departed for the interior in what was known as the Great Trek.

Bloody battles with the black indigenous groups ensued, but eventually the Boers defeated the Zulus in 1838 and set up their first republic in KwaZulu-Natal. Four years later it was annexed by the British. The Boers farther north and west had more success in claiming land for themselves. In 1852 the Transvaal Republic was founded and later the Orange Free State.

THE WAR YEARS

At the end of the 19th century tension escalated when the Boers refused to grant political rights to the British mining population in Witwatersrand. On October 11, 1899, the Anglo—Boer War broke out. The Boers held their ground throughout most of the 32 months of conflict, but the British force of nearly 500,000 soldiers proved to be too much. The Boers eventually negotiated for peace and the Peace Treaty of Vereeniging (Fir-EEN-i-GHIN) was signed on May 31, 1902, transforming the Transvaal and Orange Free State republics into British colonies again.

In 1910 the British Parliament approved the formation of the Union, making South Africa a self-governing dominion within the British Commonwealth. Louis Botha became South Africa's first prime minister. The republic was based on the parliamentary system, but blacks could only become representatives if they were nominated by whites.

During World War I South Africa joined forces with Britain and the Allies and drove the Germans out of southwestern Africa (today's Namibia). South African forces also fought in Flanders and in East Africa.

When Botha died in 1919 Jan Christiaan Smuts became prime minister. When World War II broke out, Smuts persuaded the country to declare war on Germany. Starting with only 20,000 soldiers, he managed to assemble 350,000 by 1945.

South African soldiers helped defeat the Italian army in Ethiopia during the early stages of the war. In 1941 two infantry divisions fought as part of the British Eighth Army in the Sahara Desert. They took part in the courageous stand at the Libyan port of Tobruk, where they almost stopped Germany's famed Afrika Korps.

Smuts was made an honorary field marshal of the British army in 1941. Following World War II he became a leading figure in the formation of the United Nations.

BLACK AND WHITE

In 1948 Smuts was ousted by the National Party led by Daniel F. Malan, who introduced apartheid to ensure the protection, maintenance, and consolidation of the white minority so as to dominate the black majority.

On May 31, 1961, white South Africa voted for independence from Britain, became a republic, and cut ties with the Commonwealth. That year Malan's successor, Hendrik Verwoerd, tightened apartheid policy. He was against racial mixing and wanted blacks to live in Homelands separated from the whites.

TRUTH AND RECONCILIATION COMMISSION

The Truth and Reconciliation Commission (TRC) was set up in South Africa at the end of the apartheid era to help all South Africans deal with the violence and human rights abuses that had been carried out by both sides—the apartheid government and all those involved in the fight for freedom—for more than three decades.

The point of the Commission was to let people know the truth of what had happened during those dark years in the country's history, understand what had driven people to behave in this way, and learn to forgive each other. In this way the country would be able to go forward on its new multicultural and democratic path to the future in a more peaceful way. It would be the "rainbow nation," as Nelson Mandela called it.

The role of the TRC was to hear as much evidence as it could from as many people as possible, place blame on those who were guilty, and also grant them amnesty. It would also decide who would get paid some form of compensation for their losses during this period. For example, when the main income earner in a family had died in the violence, the family could get a payment that would help them get on with their lives in the new nation. The Commission began its work in April 1996 and the final report was handed to the government in March 2003.

In protest the African National Congress (ANC) and the Pan Africanist Congress (PAC) campaigned against the unfair treatment of blacks. The government reacted harshly. Blacks were killed, tortured, and imprisoned, and organizations such as the ANC and PAC were outlawed.

The rest of the world was outraged. Countries such as the United States and the United Kingdom imposed sanctions, bans, boycotts, and restrictions, and severed ties with South Africa. The United Nations made it clear that apartheid would not be tolerated. The South African government responded brutally. Military operations were intensified, all anti-apartheid organizations were banned, and many blacks were detained without trial. These measures entrenched the unfair policies further.

SOUTH AFRICA AFTER APARTHEID

For three decades South Africa suffered under the oppression of apartheid. On February 2, 1990, the country's president, F. W. de Klerk, declared that apartheid would be dismantled and the ban on groups such as the ANC would be lifted. Political prisoners, including ANC leader Nelson Mandela, were freed and most racial laws and restrictions were removed.

A negotiating council was formed with representation from all the different political groups and races. An interim government was established and a new constitution was developed. In April 1994 all South Africans voted for the country's first-ever democratic government. On May 10 that year Nelson Mandela became the first legitimate president of South Africa.

Today South Africa is accepted internationally and admired for the way it has changed and moved forward as a democracy. It has rekindled its relationships with the many countries that had boycotted it in the past and now has diplomatic ties with most countries in the world, most notably China and all the African nations.

South Africa is a member of the African Union, formerly the Organization of African Unity, an international organization that promotes cooperation among the independent nations of Africa. It is active in the NEPAD. This brainchild of five African leaders, including South Africa's Thabo Mbeki, aims to relieve high poverty levels and develop economies in Africa by committing member countries to good governance, respect for human rights, working for peace, and poverty relief.

> "A commission is a necessary exercise to enable South Africans to come to terms with their past on a morally accepted basis and to advance the cause of reconciliation."
> —Dullah Omar, former Minister of Justice

INTERNET LINKS

www.sahistory.org.za/

This website contains interesting articles and photographs of many key events in the history of South Africa.

www.nelsonmandela.org/

This site is dedicated to the life, times, and achievements of Nelson Mandela.

www.au.int/

This is the official website of the African Union, with links to sections on its history and development, and vision and mission.

GOVERNMENT

The Union Building in Pretoria, one of the most popular tourist attractions in the city. The building is made up of east and west wings, representing the English and Boerish populations respectively.

3

THE REPUBLIC OF SOUTH AFRICA
has a democratic government. After
the first elections in 1994, President
Nelson Mandela ruled the country for
five years in accordance with its new
constitution. The ANC Party held the
majority in the national and most of
the provincial and local governments,
but other opposition parties were also
democratically represented.

The second fully democratic elections were held in 1999. Again the ANC
won the majority of seats across the country. However, Mandela decided
to step down, and Thabo Mbeki took over as the second legitimate
president of South Africa. Mbeki resigned in 2008 after losing a power
struggle to Jacob Zuma. Zuma won the presidency of the ANC and was
elected president of South Africa in 2009.

NATIONAL GOVERNMENT

The government of South Africa is made up of three separate parts:
executive (Cabinet), the legislature (Parliament), and the judiciary
(Courts of Law). The rights of the people are guarded by the constitution.
There are three tiers of government: national, provincial, and local.

Members of the National Assembly and the Senate met as a body called the Constitutional Assembly to write a new constitution that was adopted in 1996 after two years of public consultation and much debate. The constitution lays the foundation for a society based on fundamental human rights, democratic values, and social justice.

CONSTITUTION In 1996 South Africa adopted its constitution, which gives every citizen rights and obligations. These are enshrined in the Bill of Rights, which is a body of law that protects every citizen's rights. The constitution is the highest law of the land, and not even the president or parliament can pass a law that goes against it.

CABINET After elections the parliament chooses a new president who appoints the deputy president and a minister to head each government department. The president and ministers form the cabinet. It is their responsibility to run the country, but they cannot make laws.

PARLIAMENT The Parliament has two houses—the National Assembly and the National Council of Provinces (NCOP), whose members are elected by the people of South Africa. Each house has its own powers and functions. The constitution says that the National Assembly must have no more than 400 and no fewer than 350 members of parliament (MPs). They are elected through a system called proportional representation, where candidates are elected in proportion to the number of votes the party wins in the election. The president and his ministers are accountable to the Parliament. MPs draw up the laws that govern the lives of South Africans and must discuss and debate government policy and other political issues. The parliament makes the laws, but the courts, which are independent of the government, punish the lawbreakers.

NATIONAL ASSEMBLY The National Assembly is responsible for choosing the president, passing laws, and ensuring that the members of the executive perform their work properly. It also provides a forum where the representatives of the people can publicly debate issues. The NCOP debate all the bills that the Parliament draws up and can approve, reject, or change them before they are made into law. It ensures that provincial interests are taken into account in the national sphere of government. The National Assembly is also the place where ministers must report on the work they do and answer questions about their work.

THE JUDICIARY The judiciary is made up of the Constitutional Court, the Supreme Court of Appeal, High Courts, Magistrates' Courts, and other courts established or recognized through an act of Parliament. The Chief Justice of South Africa is the head of the Constitutional Court. Members of the judiciary are not elected but appointed, and they function independently because neither the government nor the individual is allowed to interfere in the work of the judiciary. It is the responsibility of the courts to try people who are accused of breaking the law and, if defendants are found guilty, to sentence them to punishment. The Constitutional Court has the power to decide whether the government is acting against the constitution or whether the Parliament has made a law that is unconstitutional.

INDEPENDENT ELECTORAL COMMISSION The Independent Electoral Commission (IEC) was established to control the election process and to ensure that every election—national, provincial, or local—is free and fair so that South Africa remains a truly democratic country.

The Western Cape High Court, which has general jurisdiction over the western cape area.

PROVINCIAL GOVERNMENT

THE NATIONAL COUNCIL OF PROVINCES One of the two houses of the Parliament, the NCOP was created to ensure that provinces and local governments have a direct voice in the Parliament when national laws are made. The council consists of delegations from the nine provinces as well as one representing all the local governments.

PROVINCIAL POWERS South Africa's nine provinces hold joint powers with the central government in matters of national administration and regional autonomy over provincial affairs. Each province has a legislature of between 30 and 100 elected members, with the actual number based on proportional representation. The local legislatures elect a premier, who heads a cabinet. The size of the cabinet also depends on proportional representation.

Children proudly show their support for Jacob Zuma. His party, ANC, won the 2009 general elections. Shortly after, he was elected the President of South Africa.

LOCAL GOVERNMENT

MUNICIPALITIES Residents of each town or city elect a municipal council that is responsible for running the municipality and providing all the services that make it work, such as garbage collection, water supply, and electricity, as well as running the town or city. About half of the municipal councillors are elected directly by the people in the area they serve and the other half are chosen based on proportional representation—in much the same way as it is done for the Parliament.

POLITICAL PARTIES AND OTHER POLITICAL ORGANIZATIONS

There are about 18 to 20 political parties in South Africa, with about 13 usually represented in the Parliament. This number is not constant because there are only three or four larger political parties, so the smaller ones often combine to get a bigger supporter base.

There are electoral rules for all parties, as administered by the IEC. After the elections only parties that get 10 percent or more of the vote are eligible to have members in the Parliament, with the actual number being dependent on proportional representation. The majority vote winner from each constituency also becomes a member of the Parliament.

Usually only a few of the larger parties hold most of the seats in the Parliament. Despite this, almost all political views, from conservative to moderate to liberal, are reflected at some level.

AFRICAN NATIONAL CONGRESS Formed in 1912 this is the largest and most popular political party. The ANC declared that its aim was to bring together all Africans as one people to defend their rights and freedoms. When it was banned in 1960, the ANC embarked on a guerrilla war against the government. The ban was lifted in 1990, when the ANC, represented by Nelson Mandela, began talks with the white government. Mandela was the party leader during the 1994 democratic elections and became the president of the country.

NEW NATIONAL PARTY (NNP) Originally this was called the National Party, an all-white organization that ruled under apartheid. It later amended its policies and was supported by all South Africans, both black and white. This party was led by F. W. de Klerk, and while he was president, he released Mandela from prison and declared the end of apartheid. In 2005 the NNP's national executive council took a unanimous vote to disband the party. Most of its previous representatives joined the ANC.

A statue of Nelson Mandela, South Africa's most influencial leader, was erected outside the Drakenstein Correctional Centre, where he spent the last three years of his 27-year prison sentence for campaigning against apartheid.

DEMOCRATIC ALLIANCE (DA) This party was the result of a joining of forces between the Democratic Party and the NNP. The NNP withdrew from this pact in 2001 and was disbanded in 2004. Helen Zille is the party leader, and the DA increased its share of the vote from about 10 percent in 1999 to 16.6 percent in 2009. Although it is not very large, the DA sees its role as challenging the ruling party and forming an opposition that speaks up about anything it feels is unjust.

In 1994, when South Africa had its first democratic election, the country had two national anthems. One was "Die Stem van Suid-Afrika," or "The Call of South Africa," from the past ruling party. It was written by C. J. Langenhoven in 1918 and set to music by Reverend M. L. de Villiers in 1921. The English translation was accepted in 1952.

The other anthem, which most people who opposed apartheid used, was "Nkosi Sikelel' iAfrika" or "Lord Bless Africa" in the Xhosa language. This was written and composed in 1897 by Enoch Sontonga, a Tembu tribesman who was also a Methodist mission school teacher. The words of the first stanza were originally written as a hymn in the Xhosa language. The original version had only one verse, but several more were added in later years by the poet Samuel Mqhayi. In 1942 a version in Sesotho was published by Moses Mphahlele. "Nkosi Sikelel' iAfrika" was sung in concerts in Johannesburg by Reverend J. L. Dube's Ohlange Zulu Choir and became a popular church hymn that was later adopted as an anthem at political meetings. It was sung as an act of defiance during the apartheid years. In 1997 shortened versions of the two anthems were joined together to become the national anthem of South Africa. The first verse is usually sung in Xhosa or Zulu followed by the Sesotho version. The third verse is in Afrikaans and the final verse is sung is English.

Nkosi sikelel' iAfrika
Maluphakanyisw' uphondo lwayo,
Yizwa imithandazo yethu,
Nkosi sikelela, thina lusapho lwayo.

Morena boloka setjhaba sa heso,
O fedise dintwa le matshwenyeho,
O se boloke, O se boloke setjhaba sa heso,
Setjhaba sa South Afrika—South Afrika.

Uit die blou van onse hemel,
Uit die diepte van ons see,
Oor ons ewige gebergtes,
Waar die kranse antwoord gee,

Sounds the call to come together,
And united we shall stand,
Let us live and strive for freedom,
In South Africa our land.

CONGRESS OF THE PEOPLE (COPE) The COPE is a new party formed by breakaway ANC members that contested its first election in April 2009, winning 7.42 percent of the vote. One of its founding members is Mosiuoa

Lekota, the former minister of defense who resigned from the Cabinet after Mbeki stepped down.

INKATHA FREEDOM PARTY (IFP) This party is led by Zulu chief Mangosuthu Buthelezi and is supported by a large number of Zulu people, especially those from the KwaZulu-Natal province. It is one of the stronger opposition parties in the Parliament.

INDEPENDENT DEMOCRATS (ID) The ID is one of South Africa's newest mainstream political parties. It was formed under the leadership of Patricia de Lille in 2003.

Other smaller but active parties include the PAC and the South African Communist Party (SACP). There are also a number of political organizations in South Africa. They are not political parties and are not represented in the Parliament, but they have strong support. One such organization is the Congress of South African Trade Unions (COSATU), the umbrella body for all major trade unions in the country.

INTERNET LINKS

www.gov.za/
This is the official website of the South African government, with detailed information on speeches and statements, government leaders, events, and policy.

www.eisa.org.za/WEP/souiec.htm
This is the official website of the independent Electoral Institute for the Sustainability of Democracy in Africa (EISA).

www.anc.org.za/show.php?id=206
This is the official website of the African National Congress (ANC), with information on its history, constitution, structure, and campaigns.

ECONOMY

The N1 highway is the main road linking Johannesburg and Cape Town. It extends all the way to Beit Bridge on the border with Zimbabwe.

4

U NTIL THE END OF THE 19th century South Africa was an agricultural country. The discovery of gold and diamonds triggered a need to invest in mining and machinery and propelled South Africa into becoming the major industrial power in Africa.

THE MODERN AGE

For most of the 1900s South Africa's economy rode on the back of gold, coal, and other mineral exports. The country produced more than half of the world's gold, enabling it to import goods it did not produce. Adequate iron ore and wealth from its gold supply allowed it to establish iron and steel industries. Other industries such as manufacturing, construction, and financial services soon developed. Toward the end of the 20th century anti-apartheid foreign sanctions strained the economy, but democratic change in 1994 opened the world to South Africa's minerals and its wide range of agricultural and manufactured products.

The new government's business policies have helped the economy grow while keeping inflation rates reasonably low. Because South Africa is again a player in the global business environment, it has been able to expand its exports for the benefit of all its people.

COMMUNITY DEVELOPMENT

More and more South Africans are moving from the farms to the towns and cities to work, especially since apartheid was dismantled. This has

South Africa has a large supply of natural resources and well-developed financial, communications, legal, energy, and transportation sectors. Modern infrastructure supports an effective distribution of goods throughout the country. The stock exchange is the 18th largest in the world.

An informal settlement in Durban. People living in these areas are more susceptible to illnesses and diseases due to lack of sanitation and the unavailability of dedicated public health services.

meant that there is not enough regular housing for everyone, especially for those who are not able to afford a proper place to stay. In an effort to resolve the urban housing shortage, the government is building a large number of new houses each year, especially for low-income families.

In the meantime many people build informal homes on the outskirts of the towns and cities using any scrap material they can find, including wooden planks, metal sheeting, and plastic. Living in informal settlements is not easy, as often there is no running water or electricity and living conditions are very crowded.

In 2010 it was estimated that 10 percent of South Africa's 44 million people lived in informal settlements. Many of these settlements have no access to running water, electricity, or facilities for basic sanitation and solid waste removal. Living conditions in these settlements are very poor, with residents facing daily challenges including fire hazards, safety and security risks, and health hazards. As the economy grows and people earn higher wages—and with some help from the government—it is hoped that regular houses will completely replace informal settlements.

RESEARCH

South Africa has a wide variety of plants and animals, a wealth of mineral resources, and a kaleidoscope of ethnic groups. This makes it a natural laboratory that offers unique opportunities for research. The country's scientists are the technological leaders of the continent, and their work has benefited people and industries throughout the world.

Research in South Africa is funded jointly by the government and businesses. This allows various organizations to conduct research in almost every field.

Major national research centers include the Council for Scientific and Industrial Research (CSIR), which conducts studies and research in the development of science and technology; the Human Sciences Research

Council of South Africa (HSRC), which concentrates on areas such as human resources and education; and the SA Medical Research Council (MRC), whose main aim is to improve national health care.

There are also a number of other research agencies in South Africa. Some are linked to the many universities in the country, which are doing work at an international level in areas such as mining, agriculture, science, housing development, and medicine.

TRANSPORTATION

Over the years South Africa has developed the best transportation network on the continent. Since 1936 highways and roads have connected all the major cities in the country.

Transportation in South Africa is provided by both the government and the private sector. Transnet is a large government-owned corporation responsible for delivering thousands of tons of goods around South Africa through its pipelines, and both to and from its ports. Transnet is made up of five operating divisions: Transnet freight rail, Transnet rail engineering, Transnet national ports authority, Transnet port terminals, and Transnet pipelines.

Private companies build, run, and collect tolls on some roads and are involved in running both passenger buses and heavy cargo trucks. They also operate some terminals in the seaports.

The rich buy their own cars. Those who cannot afford a car use the minibus taxis, which carry about 12 to 15 people at a time and offer a quick and fairly inexpensive service. The minibus taxis do not have specific pick-up or drop-off points but will stop almost anywhere. Transnet's large railroad network ferries millions of passengers throughout the country each year. It also carries cargo, especially products such as coal and iron ore, to the

People in Soweto queue to board a minibus taxi, the most available mode of transport in the country. The fares charged are very cheap, however, the drivers have a reputation of being reckless when on the road.

A worker prepares material for the production of clothing in a factory. It is the most labor-intensive segment of the manufacturing industry.

seaports for export. Some landlocked African countries such as Botswana and Zimbabwe also use South Africa's railroads and seaports to import and export goods.

MANUFACTURING

South Africa has a growing manufacturing industry that is dominated by the agriprocessing, automotive, chemicals, metals, textiles, clothing, and footwear industries. Agriculture contributes 4 percent to South Africa's gross domestic product (GDP). It is made up mostly of sheep and cattle farming, with 13 percent of land used for crops. The crops grown are corn, wheat, oats, sugarcane, and sunflowers. Car manufacturing is a large business for both local demand and export. The industry is one of South Africa's most important manufacturing sectors, with many of the major multinationals using South Africa to source components and assemble vehicles for both the international and local markets.

Private enterprise is encouraged, but there is still a substantial amount of government ownership and financial subsidizing in the manufacturing industry. The state-run Industrial Development Corporation (IDC) was set up to promote economic growth and provides finances for major projects in oil production, phosphate extraction, and the production of pulp for rayon. It also helps to finance manufacturing projects near the Homelands that attract minimal interest and are therefore limited in their potential for growth.

MINING

South Africa is a world leader in mining and is the world's largest producer of platinum and one of the leading producers of gold, diamonds, base metals, and coal. South Africa possesses the world's largest known reserves of gold, platinum-group metals, chrome ore, and manganese ore, and the second-

CAR MANUFACTURING SECTOR

South Africa has a large vehicle manufacturing industry, mostly located near Port Elizabeth and East London ports in the Eastern Cape province, and also near Pretoria in the center of Gauteng province. Nearly all the global manufacturers, including Ford, General Motors, Mercedes-Benz, Toyota, Volkswagen, and Nissan, have plants in South Africa, and together made more than 630,000 vehicles in 2008. The automotive sector contributes about 7.5 percent to the country's GDP and employs approximately 36,000 people.

In the past vehicles were made mostly for the local market, but more and more are being made for export and already nearly half the vehicles made are being exported around the world.

largest reserves of zirconium, vanadium, and titanium. The mining sector includes all five of the major mineral categories: precious metals and minerals, energy minerals, nonferrous metals and minerals, industrial minerals, and ferrous minerals.

Gold has played an important role in South Africa's economy. It is estimated that more than 50 percent of the world's gold reserves are found in South Africa. The Witwatersrand Basin yields 96 percent of South Africa's gold output and holds the world's largest-known gold reef deposit. When the price of gold skyrocketed in the 1970s, gold mining became an even more profitable venture. In 2012 more than 142,000 people were employed in the gold mining industry of South Africa.

The recent rapid rise in the world price of platinum has made platinum mining in South Africa very profitable. The country has more than 80 percent of the world's platinum group metal deposits and is expected to be a major producer for many years to come.

Coal accounts for a large portion of South Africa's mining industry. Much of the coal is used locally to generate electricity, meeting about 88 percent of South Africa's primary energy needs. In addition to the use of coal in the domestic economy, about 28 percent of South Africa's coal production is exported internationally. South Africa is the fourth-largest coal-exporter in the world.

CHANGES IN THE MINING INDUSTRY

In the past, under the old government, all of South Africa's mining industry was controlled by a fairly small number of big, white-owned mining companies, although most of the mine workers who labored underground in the mines were black. After the democratic elections in 1994, the government started to spread the wealth of the mining industry across a far wider group of people and companies. A new mining law was passed in 2003 to help this change take place. Now any new mining companies that are developed must have a fair proportion of black senior management and black shareholders.

There are already a good number of new mining companies that have been developed in this way and many of the older, well-developed, and established mining companies have diversified their businesses as well.

The junior mining sector in South Africa was the result of new legislation in the form of the Mining and Petroleum Resources Development Act of 2002. The law enforced a "use it or lose it" principle. Mining rights not used by mining companies to recover minerals in the ground would revert to the state. It then "rents" them out to companies that want to explore and mine minerals. In the past private individuals and companies could own the mineral rights, even if they did not actually mine the property. This blocked the chances of other people being able to mine many areas.

In 2009 coal became the biggest component of South Africa's mining industry by sales value, followed by platinum group metals and then gold. These top three minerals accounted for 71.2 percent of South Africa's total mineral sales.

Uranium, processed as a by-product of gold and copper mining, is exported to countries that use it in nuclear power plants. The first uranium treatment facility in South Africa was established in 1951.

South Africa produces 5 percent of the world's diamonds and is ranked seventh in the world in terms of rough diamond production. The Kaapvaal Craton in central South Africa has one of the richest diamond-bearing kimberlite dikes in the world. Most of South Africa's diamonds are mined from the ground in the area around Kimberley in the Northern Cape province, but there are good diamond deposits in Limpopo province, Gauteng province, in the oceans, and off the country's western coast. At least 90 percent of the diamonds mined in South Africa are exported.

Iron ore, zinc, tin, lead, phosphate, and vermiculite are among the other minerals mined in South Africa. More than 80 percent of the mined minerals are exported. South Africa's exports include 50 different types of commodities; the most important are gold, coal, platinum, diamonds, iron ore, copper, manganese, asbestos, nickel, zinc, tin, lead, phosphate, and vermiculite. The country's huge deposits of iron ore have allowed it to be self-sufficient in the production of steel.

Despite safety precautions, about 50,000 miners have been killed since the beginning of the 20th century. South Africa mines at depths of 2.4 miles (3.86 km)—deeper than any other country—and has a safety record that is superior to most countries. In 2010, 128 people were killed in mines in South Africa, down from 270 in 2003. The government is committed to increasing safety for mine workers.

South Africa's mining industry provides hundreds of thousands of jobs. However, the work is very dangerous and the pay is not very high. As a result many South Africans are reluctant to work in the mining industry, so mine workers have to be recruited from neighboring states.

Despite abundant mineral wealth, international trade still plays a very important role. The country imports heavy machinery, electronic equipment, and trucks. South Africa is also dependent on foreign nations for oil.

FISHING

South Africa has a strong fishing industry. Its location at the tip of the continent gives fishing boats access to both the Atlantic and Indian oceans,

An underground worker at a gold mine searches for valuable ore. In recent years, production of gold has been declining, leading to the loss of many jobs in the sector.

More than 600,000 tons of fish were produced in 2012 and the industry contributed 0.5 percent of the country's GDP.

which are teeming with marine life. More than 1,000 varieties of sea creatures, including hake, mackerel, anchovy, herring, horse mackerel, West Coast Rock lobster, and the Patagonian toothfish, are found off the coast of South Africa. The Benguela Current begins as a northward flow off the Cape of Good Hope, and then cuts through the waters to the west, where almost 80 percent of the nation's annual catch is made.

Since 1994 smaller companies and individuals have been participating in the fishing industry, which used to be controlled by large companies.

TOURISM

South Africa's tourism industry has boomed since positive reports about the post-apartheid South Africa have filtered to the rest of the world. It has become a popular tourist destination. The Department of Tourism actively promotes and develops tourism, and the sector is continuing to grow. Direct and indirect tourism's contribution to the country's GDP was 8.6 percent in 2011.

Visitors to South Africa have a number of options ranging from magnificent beaches to some of the world's most famous game parks and nature reserves. There are massive mountain ranges guarding verdant valleys, vast inland plains, forests, and waterfalls. Many mineral and hot springs are also found in South Africa.

The nation's controlled tourism industry puts wilderness to work without destroying it. Environmentally conscious tourists will be pleasantly surprised by South Africa's well-preserved natural landscape, and people are flocking to the country for safari tours. To cater to the expanding tourism industry, the government has developed efficient road, rail, and air transportation systems.

AGRICULTURE

In the past South Africa's commercial agriculture was run by large-scale farmers. Since the country's first democratic elections in 1994 there has been a move to encourage and help small-scale farmers. In this way more people, especially blacks, are getting involved. South Africa still has a dual agricultural economy with well-developed commercial farming and more subsistence-based agriculture in the rural areas. The biggest problem for agriculture in South Africa is the lack of enough water in many areas. Only 13 percent of South Africa's total land area is suitable for crop production, and only 22 percent of this is suitable arable land.

Corn is the most valuable crop, as it is the staple food of the black population. Wheat is grown mainly in the southwest, which receives the most rainfall. Other crops such as oats, sugarcane, sunflowers, rye, barley, tobacco, peanuts, and sorghum are also cultivated but to a lesser extent.

Fruit is the second most valuable crop. Although citrus fruit is not native to South Africa, most varieties are grown successfully. Vineyards are also important to South Africa's agriculture and most are located within a 150-mile (241.4-km) radius of Cape Town. KwaZulu-Natal has been producing large quantities of sugarcane since 1870. Its humid climate makes it suitable for growing subtropical fruit, which can also be found in Mpumalanga province. Today South Africa is self-sufficient in nearly all agricultural products. It is among the world's top five exporters of avocados, grapefruit, tangerines, plums, pears, and table grapes.

Rows of grape vines planted at a vineyard. Wine in South Africa has gone through a revolutionary increase in quality the past 10 to 15 years, and the industry's outlook is still promising.

Dairy products, ostrich meat, wine, hides and skins, sugar, fruit juice, wool, apples, pears, peaches, apricots, and pineapples are produced both for the domestic market and for export. South Africa's main export market is Europe and its counter-seasonality is a competitive advantage. It also has significantly shorter shipping times to Europe than other counter-seasonal countries.

Traditional cattle farmers have large herds because livestock is regarded as a measure of wealth. Many traditional farmers are turning to commercial farming, with help from the government and foreign aid organizations that help individuals obtain grazing land. However, the droughts in recent years and a decline in grazing land have taken their toll on cattle farmers.

UNIONS

Since 1924 white trade unions have had extensive and well-defined rights. This did not extend to blacks or their unions until the 1980s. In the 1980s black unions, which tended to be political, became powerful and eventually won full bargaining rights. Before the 1994 elections some of the black and white unions merged.

The new government rewrote labor laws, giving workers fair work and pay conditions. Unions now have no race distinction and accept members from almost all economic sectors. Only those working at very top management levels are not encouraged to join unions because of a possible conflict of interest.

There are a number of very powerful unions, especially in the mining, transportation, and automobile manufacturing industries. Recently, with improved work and pay conditions, there are fewer strikes.

The COSATU is in an alliance with the ANC and the SACP. In 1990, when political organizations were unbanned, the ANC, SACP, and COSATU agreed to work together as a Revolutionary Alliance (Tripartite Alliance). The Alliance is centered around goals of the National Democratic Revolution—the establishment of a nonracial and democratic South Africa, economic reforms, and the continued process of economic and political democratization.

THE WORKFORCE

A lot of work in South Africa is still not mechanized, meaning that thousands are employed in manual work, especially in the mining and agricultural sectors. Most manual laborers do not have much education and are unskilled or semi-skilled. The government is trying to improve the accessibility and quality of education so that people will be able to do more skilled work in the future.

In the past most middle- and senior-level people in business and industry were white, while most low-level workers were black. This is changing as new laws ensure that the whole workforce, from company executives to regular workers, is more representative of the entire spectrum of people in the country, most of whom are non-Caucasians.

Laws now ensure that women are treated equally in the workplace. The South African government has one of the highest percentages of women in politics and government in the world. The business community is slowly following this lead. Laws are also in place to force companies to employ people of all races if they do not do so willingly.

WORKING CONDITIONS

Now that apartheid has been dismantled, South African labor laws have instituted minimum wages, fair working conditions, and good labor practices for all workers in the country. This is especially important for the less skilled, such as farm workers and domestic workers, who in the past were paid very low wages and worked hard for long hours. It also ensures that women are given the same treatment as men.

If workers feel they have been unfairly treated, and especially unfairly dismissed, they have the right to take their case against their employer to the Commission for Conciliation, Mediation and Arbitration (CCMA), where both parties will be heard and fairly judged. The CCMA was established under the terms of the Labour Relations Act of 1995.

INTERNET LINKS

www.ngopulse.org/node/13699

This website with a wide range of online resources to highlight development issues in South Africa.

www.projectsiq.co.za/default.htm

This website contains information on mining in Africa, including detailed sections on gold and platinum mining in South Africa.

www.miningsafety.co.za/dynamiccontent/61/Mining-Safety-in-South-Africa

This is an interesting website about mining safety in South Africa, with statistics, photos, and sections on gear and clothing, machinery, and training.

ENVIRONMENT

A cactus nursery in Worcester, Western Cape.

5

IN THE EARLY YEARS of South Africa's colonial history, especially in the 18th and early 19th centuries, very little environmental conservation or preservation was carried out. This was mainly because not much was known about the concept at the time.

There was so much hunting in the country, not simply as a means of getting food but also for sport, that hundreds of thousands of animals were slaughtered. As the world changed and saw how the natural environment was being destroyed, leaders in South Africa realized that the conservation of animals and plants and their habitats was essential. For more than a century South Africa has been actively conserving and trying to protect its abundant natural plant and animal life and original terrain in a wide variety of game parks and conservation areas.

The largest and most famous game park is the 7,772-square-mile (20,129-square-km) Kruger National Park that was set up in 1898 to preserve the wildlife and natural environment of South Africa's Lowveld region. The park spans the low grassland region in the Limpopo and Mpumalanga provinces and is home to an impressive number of species: 147 mammals, 507 birds, 114 reptiles, 34 amphibians, 49 fish, and 336 trees.

Today the government, working through its Department of Environmental Affairs and Tourism, continues the process of environmental conservation. It is constantly updating its policies and approach to conservation in line with world trends. This will enable it to continuously preserve South Africa's natural heritage for all future

The environmental face of South Africa has changed dramatically over the last century. Large areas of natural vegetation have been replaced by forestry, agriculture, and urban development. Mining has altered entire landscapes. The population has shifted from a predominantly rural lifestyle to an increasingly urban lifestyle so that growing urban conglomerations are encroaching on a sizable area of the country that used to be undeveloped and uninhabited.

generations at home and around the world. The government is also working to engage the population in both caring for and living off the country's natural riches without damaging them.

INCLUDING PEOPLE

Early conservation was done mostly by not allowing the people living near a game park to use it in any way other than paying to visit the park. That led to conflicts because the neighboring communities who lived off the land did not feel like part of the process. Poaching and illegal hunting were also persistent problems.

South African National Parks has been entrusted to oversee and manage the country's 21 state-owned national game parks. Its policy follows the modern view that the successful long-term management of the parks depends greatly on the cooperation and support of the local people. Now parks and communities benefit from each other. For example the people can sell their handicrafts in the parks so that tourists get a taste of South Africa's art as well as its wildlife.

A herd of zebras graze on a grassy plain in Kruger National Park.

BIODIVERSITY

Biodiversity, the wide variety of plants and animals and their environments, is considered a national asset as important as diamonds or gold. Environmental conservation is of great importance. There is a lot of pressure on the natural environment from a growing human population, farming, deforestation, and other activities. South Africa contains an estimated 10 percent of the world's known bird, fish, and plant species, and

A pangolin, or scaly anteater, in the Northern Cape of South Africa.

more than 6 percent of the world's mammal and reptile species. At present there are a number of threatened species of plants and animals that need additional protection. There are 17 threatened species in South Africa, including the black rhino, pangolin, and giant golden mole. The riverine rabbit, roan antelope, and wild dog are endangered. The blue antelope and the quagga have become extinct.

On a practical level one of the great advantages of conserving biodiversity is the continuance of many medicines that are made from plants found only in South Africa. There are more than 20,000 flowering plants in South Africa. Some of the plants are used in modern medical science, while others are used by the *sangomas* or traditional healers, and herbalists.

TRANSFRONTIER PARKS

South Africa shares a few transfrontier, or cross-border, parks with its neighbors. By joining separate parks together, huge wilderness areas can be formed that are better geared for sustainable wildlife conservation.

When transfrontier parks are set up, there are no man-made boundaries within them. The animals are able to roam freely and naturally, as they did before people created borders around tracts of land to mark out their respective countries. It also means that visitors to the parks are able to move

The Kgalagadi Transfrontier Park in Botswana was set up to protect the migrating oryx, or gemsbok, from poachers.

freely within these very large areas and get a true feeling of what the great wilderness is like.

One of the largest initiatives that South Africa is involved in is the Great Limpopo Transfrontier Park. It joins conservation land and game parks in South Africa to those in Mozambique and Zimbabwe. The park is 13,437.5 square miles (34,803 square km) in size—larger than Israel. This area forms the core of the second-phase transfrontier conservation area (TFCA), measuring almost 38,610 square miles (100,000 square km)—the world's greatest animal kingdom.

The larger transfrontier conservation area will include Zinave and Banhine national parks, the Corumana and Massingir areas and interlinking regions in Mozambique, and also some privately and state-owned conservation areas in South Africa and Zimbabwe bordering on the Transfrontier Park.

In 2005 the Giriyondo Access Facility between the Kruger and Limpopo national parks was opened. Approximately 5,000 animals were moved from Kruger to Limpopo National Park. Approximately 31 miles (50 km) of fencing was removed, which has encouraged more animals to cross the border of their own accord. It is estimated that about 1,000 elephants crossed the border.

Within the park visitors will also find archaeological sites from the Stone Age and Iron Age, evidence that ancient man once roamed the wilderness of South Africa.

MARINE PROTECTED AREAS

South Africa has established Marine Protected Areas (MPAs), which are special areas set aside for protecting either one marine species or a wide variety of marine life. This usually means that no one may fish or interfere in any way with marine life in that area to keep it as close to its original natural

state as possible. This helps the protected marine habitat and its inhabitants to grow and sustain other creatures that move in and out of the area such as sharks, whales, and dolphins.

MPAs are important because overfishing has reduced the numbers of certain species of marine life to dangerously low levels. Fishermen blame MPAs for bad business, but the government remains committed to protecting the nation's natural resources for future generations. One of the larger and more beautiful MPAs in South Africa is the Tsitsikamma National Park situated at the heart of the tourist region known as the Garden Route on the southeastern coast near Plettenberg Bay. Proclaimed in 1964 the park incorporates 50 miles (80 km) of rocky coastline. It is forbidden to take anything from the area. Even fishing is prohibited so as to enable baseline research on endangered fish species in their natural environment. One of the largest single MPAs in the world, Tsitsikamma conserves 11 percent of South Africa's temperate south coast rocky shoreline.

In 2009 Mozambique and South Africa created Africa's first transfrontier marine conservation area by linking the area at Ponto do Ouro in Mozambique with South Africa's iSimangaliso Wetland Park. The protected area includes 200 miles (300 km) of shoreline and beaches of the continent's southeast

One of the largest in Africa, the De Hoop Marine Protected Area is home to an attractive diversity of marine life.

WORLD SUMMIT

The United Nations World Summit on Sustainable Development, also known as the Johannesburg Summit because it was held in Johannesburg in August 2002, brought together tens of thousands of people, including heads of state and heads of government, national delegates, and leaders from nongovernmental organizations (NGOs), businesses, and other groups. Their aim was to focus the attention of the whole world on conserving Earth's natural resources and improving the quality of life of many millions of people who do not live with the same benefits, such as running water and electricity, good jobs, and enough food, as do people in the United States, Europe, and other countries.

At the summit people from all over the world discussed the problems they faced, the possible solutions that could be found, and also what had been achieved and learned in the 10 years since the first summit, the Earth Summit held in Rio de Janeiro in 1992. They also discussed how groups, organizations, and countries could help one another, what they could learn from one another, and what could be learned from mistakes made in the past.

Apart from the main summit meetings, there were other fringe events held for a variety of NGOs, trade unions, and other groups as well as for members of the public. The United Nations was the main organizer of the Johannesburg Summit with help from a South African organization, Johannesburg World Summit Company.

coast from Maputo Bay in Mozambique to Cape Saint Lucia in South Africa. The Ponta do Oura/Kosi Bay Transfrontier Conservation Area contains sensitive breeding grounds of leatherback and loggerhead turtles that are threatened by human encroachment and uncontrolled harvesting of their eggs.

TOURISM AND ENVIRONMENTAL EDUCATION

South Africa is blessed with a variety of animals and plants, and this is one aspect of the country that attracts a growing number of visitors each year. Tourism creates jobs for many people across South Africa, especially near game parks or coastal resorts. Tourism is also very important because it helps generate money to fund conservation.

A recycling collection point in Hout Bay, categorized into tins, plastic and paper bins. The recycling rate of plastics packaging is expected to reach 35 percent by 2015.

Conservation can only be really successful when people understand what it is about and why it is necessary. Thus emphasis has been placed on teaching young South Africans about their natural heritage. For example SANParks runs programs that expose young people to the wilderness in a national park. It is hoped that they will in turn teach and inspire others in their communities.

There are also private organizations such as the Wildlife and Environment Society of South Africa (WESSA) and the Endangered Wildlife Trust (EWT), which help increase awareness and teach people how to make the least possible negative impact on the environment.

South Africa is a founding member of the Antarctic Treaty System (ATS), which dedicates the area south of the 60° latitude to peace and science. It also provides for the environmental protection and conservation of this important region in the southern parts of the oceans.

ENVIRONMENTAL AWARENESS

During the apartheid years many blacks were forced to live in separate rural areas known as Homelands. Overcrowding, lack of services, and poor environmental awareness caused massive soil erosion in these areas. Forests were destroyed for firewood, and rare animal species faced extinction because

of widespread hunting. An overdependence on coal as an energy source caused pollution levels to escalate to dangerous levels. Many international environmental organizations have criticized South Africa for creating "ecological wastelands."

In 1994 a Reconstruction and Development Program (RDP) was introduced by the new government of National Unity, led by Nelson Mandela. One of its highlights was an emphasis on land reform and environmental protection. This was to be achieved by heightening environmental awareness through education. The government also encouraged small-scale farming in rural areas and ensured that businesses adhered to international environmental standards.

South Africa's recycling campaigns and pollution control lag behind those in developed countries. Especially in the former Homelands, where many people are struggling simply to survive, environmental issues are not a priority. However, the post-apartheid government is attempting to raise the environmental consciousness of South Africans.

Solar cell panels generate electricity while the windmill pumps water from a borehole at a farm.

ELECTRICITY GENERATION

South Africa generates its own electricity mostly from coal. Even though this is the least expensive method, it is also environmentally unfriendly. Eskom, the state-owned power company, is constantly trying to improve the efficiency of power stations while at the same time reducing their pollution levels. It is also exploring more efficient and less polluting means of generating electricity, such as from natural gas.

Some electricity is generated from nuclear power. Wind power and solar energy are also important sources of electricity. To encourage and promote the widespread use of solar water heating, Eskom has rolled out a large-scale solar water heating program. This program offers assistance in the form of a financial rebate if a solar water heater is bought to replace a conventional geyser.

PLASTIC BAGS

People often jokingly call plastic bags South Africa's national flower because many discarded bags can be found strewn on the roadside in towns and cities. The bags are also found caught on wire fences and in tree branches. To reduce plastic bag litter, the government introduced a law in 2003 forbidding shops to give out plastic bags. Shops can either give out paper bags or sell customers thicker, stronger bags that can be reused.

INTERNET LINKS

www.environment.gov.za/

This is the official website of the Department of Environmental Affairs, with information covering projects and programs, policy and legislation, statutory bodies, and a calendar of events.

www.soer.deat.gov.za/State_of_the_Environment.html

This is the official website of the South African government, with detailed information pertaining to the state of the environment. Topics covered include air quality, climate, human settlements, pollution, and emerging issues.

www.wessa.org.za/

This is the official website of the Wildlife and Environment Society of South Africa (WESSA).

SOUTH AFRICANS

A family standing outside their home.

6

THE 53 MILLION CITIZENS of South Africa represent a spectrum of cultures. At one end is the urban middle class who live a modern, Western lifestyle, a group that has seen an increase in blacks since the end of the apartheid.

At the other end are the industrial workers and small-scale farmers, who are generally poor and live in small homes on the outskirts of towns and cities or in the rural areas.

The majority of South Africans—42.3 million—are blacks from different indigenous groups such as Zulu, Xhosa, and Sotho. The whites total 4.6 million and are mainly of Dutch, British, French, German, and Portuguese descent. There are about 4.8 million mixed-race, or Colored, people and 1.3 million Asians.

BLACKS

Blacks entered the country from the interior of Africa over a period of several centuries. By 1500 a group of blacks called Nguni had occupied the land for centuries. By 1651, when whites began settling in what is now South Africa, they met groups of Sotho-speaking people.

From their first meeting it was clear that blacks and whites had a different concept of land ownership. Blacks did not regard the land as private property but as a communal possession. Whites, on the other hand, overran large tracts of land to better their position and power.

Black indigenous groups were formed through a hereditary system of authority. The Zulus, one of the most prominent groups, were led

Costumed Zulus as part of a welcoming party to the Lesedi African Lodge and Cultural Village, where visitors are taken on a rich cultural experience.

by a famous leader called Shaka, who ruled the entire region now known as KwaZulu-Natal. The Zulu empire disintegrated after the arrival of the whites. A period of coexistence between the blacks and whites followed but there was no integration.

Before moving to the towns and cities built by the whites, many blacks first established themselves on farms. A large proportion still lives in the rural areas on small farms and in villages. The rural areas are often shabby and run-down, and many people are unemployed. Some homes may have no running water or electricity, but the government is trying steadily to improve living conditions. In some cases family members go to work in towns and cities and come home only a few times a year.

WHITES

The majority of South Africa's 4.5 million whites are descendants of the Dutch, German, French, and British colonists.

AFRIKANERS The Afrikaners are descendants of the Dutch, German, and French Huguenots who arrived in South Africa from the 17th century onward. The origins of this group can be traced to the pioneers of the Dutch East India Company, who settled in South Africa in 1651. By the end of 1750 they had penetrated far into the interior. They were mainly farmers, known as Boers.

In 1814 Britain began its bid for control by trying to Anglicize the 26,000 Afrikaners, but the latter remained steadfast and continued to speak Afrikaans, a simplified version of Dutch, mixed with French and German.

Afrikaners became discontent with British rule. From 1836 to 1838 about 10 percent of the population embarked on the Great Trek. They moved deeper into the interior and founded their own republics, Orange

NELSON MANDELA

Nelson Rolihlahla Mandela is the most famous South African, known across the world as the leader of the struggle for freedom and democracy in South Africa. Mandela is also known as South Africa's first democratically elected president and as a man who has stood up for justice and fairness for all people around the world, regardless of their race, religion, color, or beliefs.

Mandela was born in Mvezo, a village near Mthatha in the Transkei, on July 18, 1918, and finished his early schooling there. He completed his first university degree and began studying law when he moved to Johannesburg. At that time he became deeply involved in the struggle of black South Africans for freedom and equality. He joined the ANC in 1943, and in the 1950s he organized campaigns resisting the unfair laws made by the whites. This led to his being tried and convicted for treason, and in 1964 he was sentenced to life imprisonment at Robben Island.

At the end of his treason trial in 1964 Mandela said "I have fought against white domination, and I have fought against black domination. I have cherished the ideal of a democratic and free society in which all persons live together in harmony and with equal opportunities. It is an ideal which I hope to live for and to achieve. But if needs be, it is an ideal for which I am prepared to die."

After years of growing resistance from many South Africans and other countries in the world to the unfair and racist policies of apartheid, Mandela was released from prison in 1990 by President F. W. de Klerk. The two men jointly received the Nobel Peace Prize in 1993 for their efforts in ending the apartheid system in South Africa through a peaceful negotiated settlement.

The next year, in the first ever democratic elections in South Africa, Mandela was elected the country's first black president. This was a very meaningful event for a country that had fought against unjust laws for many decades. After his five-year term in office, he retired from South African politics. Since then he has set up three foundations bearing his name: the Nelson Mandela Centre of Memory, the Nelson Mandela Children's Fund, and the Mandela-Rhodes Foundation. He continues to travel the world, helping peace efforts in other countries.

The Boers transporting Dr. Leander Starr Jameson, who led a raid to take Johannesburg from the Transvaal government, to the British to be tried.

Free State and Transvaal, in the hope of placing themselves out of British reach. Unfortunately the republics were short-lived.

In 1872 the discovery of gold in the Lydenburg district of South Africa brought thousands of fortune-seekers, mainly from Britain. Pilgrim's Rest and Barberton were established as mining towns in this area. The large influx of British immigrants, combined with the Afrikaners' dissatisfaction with British rule, eventually led to the First Anglo—Boer War in 1880. After a long campaign the Boers were eventually defeated, and Afrikaners again came under the British rule. In 1910 the Afrikaners regained control of South Africa from Britain.

Afrikaners maintain their distinct identity to this day, but also mix with other groups.

ENGLISH-SPEAKING WHITES The British first occupied the Cape in 1795, establishing an English-speaking community.

In 1820, 5,000 Britons arrived at Port Elizabeth and settled on the surrounding land. They brought poetry and prose as well as skills in crafts, engineering, and education, contributing to the cultural heritage of the new country. Grahamstown, the center of British influence, grew into a community of learning that boasted several schools and a college. During the 19th century the British began to penetrate the interior of South Africa, eventually proclaiming Natal as a separate British province. English-speaking South Africans played a big role in the development of the business community, especially in and around Johannesburg.

JEWS The first Jewish congregation in Cape Town dates back to 1841. The first synagogue, Tikvat Israel ("Hope of Israel," referring to the Cape of Good Hope), was established eight years later in Cape Town and is still standing. Today there are about 75,000 Jews living in South Africa. Their contribution to economic, educational, and cultural life has been considerable. Jews played a large role in developing the country's business sector, and some were also active in liberal politics, pushing for democracy and the end to apartheid. There are synagogues in all of South Africa's large cities, and services are well attended during Jewish festivals. Johannesburg, Cape Town, and Durban have the largest Jewish populations.

PORTUGUESE The Portuguese can claim to have been the first white people to set eyes on South Africa. In 1488 the first explorer to sail around the Cape of Good Hope was Portuguese navigator Bartolomeu Dias, who was followed by his compatriot Vasco da Gama on his way to India in 1497. Many Portuguese came to South Africa from Angola and Mozambique after Portugal withdrew from those colonies. In fact there are about 500,000 Portuguese in South Africa today, making them the most numerous white minority in the country.

A portrait of an English-speaking white female in Cape Town.

ITALIANS Thousands of Italian soldiers captured during World War II were sent to South Africa as prisoners of war. They were well cared for and were employed on farms or in building and construction companies. After the war many opted to remain and were eventually joined by their families. They have since added their skills to the food, engineering, textile, and paper industries. Many Italians have opened restaurants, providing South Africans with an authentic taste of Italian cuisine.

GREEKS Large communities of Greeks have settled in all of South Africa's main centers, particularly Pretoria and Johannesburg, where there are Greek churches, schools, and several Greek cultural organizations. About 66 percent of the Greek community have become South African citizens. They range from businesspeople to café or shop owners.

Three Cape Malays joining in the Cape Minstrel festivities. Cape Malays possess strong cultural and religious identities.

ASIANS

There are 1.3 million Asians living in South Africa, including Indian, Chinese, Malay, and other Asian and East Asian people. The majority are of Indian descent, with many coming from India to work on the large sugar plantations of KwaZulu-Natal.

In the Cape Town area a few thousand Cape Malays, whose ancestors were brought over by the Dutch from Southeast Asia during the colonial period, still form a distinct community. But as South Africans of Asian origin, they are a minority compared to South African Indians and, to a lesser extent, South African Chinese.

The Asian population was one of the fastest-growing groups in South Africa from 1911 to 1970.

INDIANS Even though the first Indians arrived in South Africa in 1860, it was only in 1961 that they were accepted as a permanent component of South Africa's multicultural population and granted the status of full citizens. As a community Indians are not culturally homogeneous. However, their exposure to Western influences has had a marked effect on their traditional lifestyle. While the older generation continues to observe traditional Asian customs brought over from their home country, the younger generation appears to be adopting a more Western way of life.

South African Indians have had an oppressive and difficult life. They have been discriminated against by successive governments that have designated separate Indian business and residential areas. As it was with the Coloreds and blacks, during apartheid Indians were forcibly removed from certain areas and made to live in designated areas.

The Indian community accepted this unfair treatment, but not without protest and court action. They were also active in the ANC and its struggle against apartheid. Being efficient, disciplined, and hard-working businesspeople and traders has helped them greatly in overcoming discrimination. Now that apartheid is a thing of the past, Indians have begun to exercise their freedom of choice in where they live and do business.

Most of the Indian community can be found in and around Durban. There is also a large community in the Johannesburg area as well as in other major cities in the country.

Both the Islamic and Hindu faiths are practiced in the Indian community. In Durban there are some beautiful Hindu temples, and the community participates in the annual Festival of Lights, or Diwali. Many of the Indians and much of the Malay community from Cape Town as well as some of the Colored community practice the Islamic faith, worshiping at the many mosques throughout the urban areas in South Africa. They also observe the Islamic holy month of fasting, Ramadan.

English has become the first language for many Indians in South Africa. A majority of the Indians in South Africa today were born in the country. But many of them still are able to speak Tamil or Hindi, while some are even adept at speaking Afrikaans.

Indians earn a living as shoemakers in the Alexandra township.

CHINESE A shortage of black labor in the Johannesburg and Reef gold mines in the late 19th century prompted the recruitment of some 64,000 Chinese workers. They arrived soon after the Anglo—Boer War, but by 1910 most of the miners had been sent home. Members of the present Chinese community are not the descendants of the labor force that was imported in 1904. In 1891 Chinese traders began arriving, initially from Canton. In 1950 this immigration was forbidden, but Chinese continued to enter from South Africa's neighboring countries as well as from Taiwan and Singapore. Today there are about 12,000 South African Chinese living in the country, the majority in Johannesburg.

The South African Chinese population is generally fluent in English and Afrikaans. Many families, however, still communicate in their regional dialects, the most widespread of which are Hakka and Cantonese.

The Chinese continue to play an increasingly important role in the development of a modern South African society.

South African Chinese men partake in a Dragon dance as part of the Chinese New Year celebrations.

COLOREDS

The Coloreds are the mixed descendants of the Khoisan, the blacks, and the European and Asian settlers. More than 65 percent of the 4.8 million Coloreds live in what was previously known as Cape province. Largely Afrikaans-speaking, over the years they have identified primarily with the white population. During the apartheid era, however, many Coloreds sympathized with the blacks. They showed their support by petitioning to reclassify themselves as blacks and by joining anti-apartheid groups. While Coloreds had been victims of discriminatory laws in the past, they were, unlike the blacks, represented in the former government.

Subcultural groups such as the Griquas are also classified as Coloreds. The Griquas are largely of Khoikhoi-European ancestry and have developed a culture of their own. Religion and a love of sacred music and song are the main characteristics of this dwindling community, which is being assimilated into the Colored population. They have also been the victims of discriminatory laws.

The portrait of a typical person of Griquas ancestry.

INTERNET LINKS

www.voortrekker-history.co.za/blood_river_great_trek.php

This website contains detailed information on the Dutch settlers in South Africa.

www.capetown.at/heritage/history/british.htm

This site provides detailed information on the history and heritage of Cape Town, with links, audio guides, and photos.

www.ancestry24.com/the-portuguese-in-south-africa/

This site contains detailed information on the Portuguese in South Africa, from 1488 to the present day.

LIFESTYLE

Locals and tourists crowd the Clifton 4th Beach (one of four beaches in the suburb) to bask in the sun and enjoy a magnificient view of the Table Mountain.

W ITH THE DISMANTLING of apartheid South African lifestyles have changed drastically, especially for the blacks. It is estimated that by the year 2020 some 80 percent of blacks will be living in cities. Current government policy is directed at helping non-whites secure employment in government or the private sector and get a head start in business.

The whites used to have a privileged lifestyle, but this has changed. Most are finding it harder to get jobs because they have to compete with the whole population, not just other whites. The standard of living for some whites has dropped, while increasing numbers of blacks have improved theirs.

THE ILLS OF THE LAND

To understand the lifestyle of South Africans, it is necessary to know what life was like during the apartheid years. In 1948 racist laws separated blacks from whites in every sphere of life. They also made a distinction for Coloreds and Indians who were considered black, and Asians who were considered white. Notices in many places announced "whites only" or "blacks only." The social and economic life of South Africa was based on such distinctions.

7

The lifestyle of South Africans changes according to their income, their geographical position, and their preferences. South Africa is a stunningly beautiful country with a culturally diverse population and a large variety of attractions and activities to enjoy.

DIE AFDELINGSRAAD VAN DIE KAAP
HIERDIE GEBIED IS SLEGS VIR BLANKES
OP LAS SEKRETARIS
THE DIVICIONAL COUNCIL OF THE CAPE
THIS AREA FOR WHITES ONLY
BY ORDER · SECRETARY

THIS · IS· AN APARTHEID SIGN PRE · 1994

An example of a sign displayed during the apartheid years, segregating the white and black people.

A great deal of discrimination resulted, and the wide gulf that developed was a deterrent to social mixing. Some whites thought that by keeping to themselves, they would avoid being overwhelmed by the larger black population. Interracial marriages were forbidden, and each group of people had to live in separate areas. The only place they were allowed to mix was the workplace, and even there discrimination also existed.

Black people were required to carry permits or passes when they entered the city. Millions of blacks were arrested and detained without trial. A host of discriminatory laws were passed, forcing blacks to take on menial tasks and live in townships where living conditions were poor.

Anti-apartheid committees formed throughout the world in protest against the maltreatment of South African blacks. In 1960 the death of 69 blacks during a protest march at Sharpeville against carrying passes caused a worldwide outcry. The police at Sharpeville used live ammunition to disperse the unarmed crowds and an official inquiry into the incident proved that people were shot in the back as they were running away. Sanctions and boycotts began in support of South Africa's anti-apartheid groups. But the racist policies continued. Black political groups were banned, their leaders were thrown into prison, and the streets were filled with death and destruction. Poverty, misery, and large-scale unemployment overtook the country.

After decades of hardship, the government finally relented. In February 1990 it lifted the ban on all political organizations, released political prisoners, and repealed the bulk of discriminatory laws.

The 1994 democratic government abolished the last of the racist laws and discriminatory policies. Needless to say there have been problems, including an increase in the crime rate, as blacks and whites become accustomed to their new roles and to living as equals in a "rainbow nation." Most South Africans are optimistic about the future of the country, and the whites who were dissatisfied with the situation have emigrated.

BLACK LIFE

For years many blacks traveled from the Homelands to the cities to work because of the lack of jobs in their areas. Urban blacks lived in townships around major cities in small government-supplied houses or shacks made from wood, iron, and plastic. Townships were created by the white government that were, in effect, huge ghettos. Resentment against apartheid was particularly strong there as several hundred blacks died in township riots. Soweto, outside Johannesburg, was the most rebellious and notorious township. Today the new government has allocated money to upgrade the townships. The word Soweto was originally an acronym for "South Western Townships." The townships were created to house the blacks who were relocated from areas in Johannesburg that the apartheid government then reserved for whites. Soweto is still the most populated black urban residential area in the country, with more than one million residents.

In the countryside most blacks live, as they did before the Europeans came, in villages of mud and reed dwellings known as kraals. Various indigenous groups use different architectural styles for their dwellings. For instance traditional Zulu and Xhosa homes are shaped like beehives and made of mud and grass, while Ndebele huts are usually brightly painted with

Urban Blacks sitting on a bench in Soweto.

Ndebele huts painted using earth pigments. The Ndebele people used to live in grass huts but switched to mud walls in the mid-18th century, leading to the creation of the art form.

large geometric patterns. Some rural dwellers wear traditional dress made of blankets and skins adorned with bright beads and ornaments. Urban blacks have adopted Western-style clothing.

CUSTOMS Although each indigenous group has its own distinct customs, some share similar beliefs. One common custom is ancestor worship, a form of religion that is usually mediated by a traditional healer called a sangoma (sung-GAW-mah). Many indigenous groups, such as the Zulu and the Xhosa, are superstitious and believe that supernatural beings, often ancestral spirits, can cause misfortune. Their beliefs are reflected in the strict codes of honor that govern their interpersonal relations and the deep respect they hold for their elders.

Although several groups have retained their traditional culture, traditional dress made of hide and decorated with beads, and traditional rituals, many of their customs have started disappearing. Living in an ever more global and wired world means that many South Africans are adapting at least some of their lifestyle to new ways.

FUNERALS South African black funerals are unique. The ability of an individual, family, or community to give their next of kin a dignified burial is a significant cultural event. Black people form burial societies that collect money from members to ensure that in the event of a death, the family will have money to pay for the funeral.

A black funeral is regarded as a social event. Underprivileged communities combine their resources to provide food and drink for people who attend the funeral. At some black funerals there are often as many as 400 to 500 mourners present. Funerals are not somber affairs, as mourners usually sing and dance. In the past funerals were often used as political platforms, and mourners would carry protest signs if the person had died of something related to apartheid.

TOWNSHIPS Black townships developed near the major cities due to the presence of hundreds of black laborers working in the cities who were not allowed to live there. Many of the townships were no more than slums of cramped, substandard quarters without plumbing or electricity. Since 1994 the separated living areas have been scrapped. Today every citizen is entitled to live and own property anywhere in the country. In addition the government spends a large portion of its annual budget to improve conditions in the existing townships and to build houses for the millions of homeless families.

A funeral procession being held. The dead are usually brought back to their homelands for burial.

The QwaQwa homeland housed the Bakoena and Batlokoa tribes, before being abolished in 1994.

HOMELANDS In 1958, when Prime Minister Hendrik Verwoerd came to power, he tightened all apartheid policies. Although he wanted blacks to continue working in the white cities and towns, he felt that they should return to their own areas at night. He set aside certain tracts of land that were to be used by indigenous groups and called them Homelands.

To implement racial policies aimed at further separating whites and blacks, the government forcibly removed blacks from their homes and ordered them to resettle in the Homelands. Families were uprooted and often separated in the relocation. Blacks had to travel long distances to reach the cities where they worked, and many left their families to live in the townships.

The Homelands of the Transkei, Venda, Ciskei, and Bophuthatswana regions made up 13.7 percent of South Africa's land area yet accommodated more than half the population. The Homelands were plagued by overcrowding, erosion, and poor health conditions.

WHITE LIFE

Although there are a variety of cultural groups within the white community, their lifestyles are very similar. Many whites attend the church, and most are interested in sports, as either spectators or players. Whites enjoy a relatively high standard of living. Their homes, which are often luxurious, are located in city suburbs. During the apartheid years Afrikaners held most of the government and civic positions. They also controlled the agricultural sector of the economy. Today the number of Afrikaners working in these areas has decreased because of the competition with a larger number of candidates, including the blacks, for these positions.

ASIAN LIFE

The Malay community had originally settled in the Cape Town area and brought many Malay and Islamic customs with them. They have a good reputation as builders and artisans, although now they work in all areas of the economy and government. The Indian communities are mainly situated in KwaZulu-Natal. They are renowned as businesspeople and often own and run their own businesses.

Colorful traditional houses line a street in Bo-Kaap, Cape Town. The neighborhood is mostly inhabited by Cape Malays.

COLORED LIFE

Coloreds are usually compared with the white community, as their culture and values are similar. Many Coloreds are Christians, but a growing number are becoming Muslim. Many are skilled artisans, and some have entered government, business, education, and the medical profession.

HEALTH CARE

In the past health care in South Africa was excellent for whites but basic for the rest of the population, with some areas not receiving any medical care at all. People living in rural areas often had to walk many miles to the nearest clinic, which was not necessarily well equipped.

Today South Africa is trying to extend good health-care services to everyone and provide health care education that covers all the different needs. This is difficult and expensive. Many state-run hospitals and clinics do not have enough facilities, doctors, or medicine to serve the poorer people

Some public health care rendered by South African government bodies is free or charged according to the patient's means.

AIDS

Sadly one of the most difficult and important issues South Africa has to face at present is the very high percentage of people who have contracted AIDS (acquired immunodeficiency syndrome). Research suggests that 5.3 million people, about 17.5 percent of the adult population, are living with the HIV virus. This is causing many social problems across the country. In the worst cases there are children who are looking after their siblings because both their parents and sometimes all other adults in their family have died from the disease.

In 1987 the apartheid government recognized that HIV and AIDS had the potential to become a major problem in South Africa, even though there were few reported cases. In 1990 a prenatal survey was conducted, which found that only 0.87 percent of pregnant women were infected. The government ignored these early indications of the epidemic and fought growing national and international appeals for a public awareness and treatment program to save lives. By 2008 new infections were occurring at a rate of about 1,500 a day, and 1,000 deaths a day were attributed to AIDS. Barbara Hogan was appointed as health minister and immediately committed the government to a decisive response to the epidemic.

Approximately 70 percent of the caseload in the public health system is taken up by HIV and AIDS cases. Health-care workers and doctors have been overwhelmed by the impact of the epidemic on the public health service. The government has identified four priority areas: prevention; treatment, care, and support; research, monitoring, and surveillance; and human rights access to justice and law reform.

Many local, national, and international nongovernmental organizations (NGOs) have responded to the HIV and AIDS crisis that South Africa is facing. They are involved in research and education and also in care and treatment programs, human rights work, and prevention. These private organizations are doing as much as they can to both educate people on prevention of the disease, and to help those and their families who have contracted AIDS. Many South Africans, especially in the government sector, wear an AIDS ribbon pinned to their jacket or shirt to show solidarity with people who have AIDS as well as to keep reminding everyone of the importance of trying to overcome this major problem.

who use them, but the government is trying to improve this. Only the wealthy can afford the health care provided by the few private hospitals and clinics. Most doctors prefer to work in the urban areas, so the government has decreed that all newly qualified doctors must spend a year in rural areas to help with the shortages there.

The government provides free health care to young children and pregnant women and runs a national nutrition program that provides food for poorer children in primary schools.

The Phelophepa Health Care Train, also known as the "train of hope", travels to various impoverished rural villages to provide primary healthcare services. A second train was launched in 2012 in a bid to serve even more needy people.

Poverty and a shortage of food have always been a problem in South Africa. The government is taking measures to improve the situation, but it will take a long time. The nation also needs economic growth to create more jobs so that everyone can afford better food and health care.

EDUCATION

Former education policy discriminated against blacks. State-funded education facilities for whites were very good, but this was not the case for black, Colored, and Asian children. Although it was compulsory for all children to attend school from the age of seven to the age of 15, the policy was often not enforced in black schools. White South African children received a good education virtually for free, while the black children had a very basic and limited "Bantu education." The 1953 Bantu Education Act brought education under the control of the government, whereas previously many of schools were run by missionaries. Government funding for black schools was only available to schools which accepted a racially discriminatory curriculum. Many black children, especially from poor families, did not attend school regularly or never attended at all. The white government created the Bantu Education to teach African students to be "hewers of wood and drawers of water" for a white-run society, irrespective of the black child's abilities and aspirations. Education for everyone was free in government schools until 1992. Although this helped poorer children, the quality of their education was often inferior. It did not prepare them for any sort of decent job in their adult life.

Today's government is working hard to rectify the situation, and the education sector receives about 20 percent of the total state expenditure, the largest share of government spending. Much has been achieved since apartheid was scrapped, but the apartheid legacy is still apparent. The literacy rate stands at about 86 percent of the adult population, which means that about 5 million South Africans are not functionally literate adults.

The government has made it a major priority to improve literacy among all South Africans. Today every school is open to all races, and attendance is compulsory for nine years. School fees have to be paid in most schools, but the government has introduced a system that subsidizes or forgoes fees for children from families who cannot afford to pay.

Multicultural classrooms are promoted in South African education to encourage acceptance and the sharing of values among youth during the post-apartheid times.

Children are taught in English and one of the other 10 official languages. Previously they were taught in English and Afrikaans, neither of which was spoken in the homes of black children from rural area. This made lessons difficult to understand. Private schools are generally elite and charge high fees.

There are a number of universities and colleges, mostly situated in or near the major towns and cities. Fees have to be paid, but there are scholarships to help the underprivileged. They can also study part-time while they work. Almost 57 percent of whites and about 45 percent of Indians enroll in higher education. The rate for Coloreds is 14.8 percent, while blacks are even lower at 13.3 percent. Poor-quality primary and secondary schooling is considered to be the reason for this discrepancy, which the current government is addressing in its strategy "Action Plan to 2014: Towards the Realisation of Schooling 2025." This strategy aims to improve the training of teachers and implements a new curriculum with a focus on literacy and numeracy.

Students in front of Ou Hoofgebou, the University of Stellenbosch campus in Western Cape.

INTERNET LINKS

www.saweb.co.za/townships/index.html

This website contains detailed information on townships in South Africa.

www.ciskei.com/

This website provides general information and history of Ciskei.

www.info.gov.za/aboutsa/education.htm

This is an official government website, with detailed information about the education system in South Africa.

RELIGION

The elaborate interior of the Cathedral of St. Michael and St. George in Grahamstown.

ALTHOUGH NOT ALL are actively practicing Christianity, more than 79 percent of South Africans are Christians. These Christians are mostly whites and Coloreds, but also include blacks and Indians. Some blacks have adapted Christianity to better fit their needs by merging it with their belief in the power of ancestral spirits.

The Moederkerk Dutch Reformed Church is a simple and white church boasting neo-Gothic architecture.

8

The religions of South Africa are as diverse as its people. There are many different religions, including African traditional religion and the religion of the San people. These religions have their roots in South Africa. Christianity, Judaism, Islam, Hinduism, and Buddhism were imported into the country by immigrants during the last 500 years.

Other major religions in South Africa include Islam (1.5 percent), Hinduism (1.2 percent), African traditional belief (0.3 percent), and Judaism (0.2 percent). As in many urban societies, a growing number of people do not practice their religion or have no specific religion.

In the past Christian values were the main focus of the government and the media. Now all other major religions are also represented and frequently addressed in public or state gatherings with a more interdenominational approach. The constitution ensures freedom of worship for all.

Zion women of the Zionist Christian Church wear green dresses and berets as part of their uniform. The men don khaki trousers, jackets and flat-topped hats.

South Africa has a rich tradition of worship through music, especially choral music. There are many choirs that sing mostly religious music unaccompanied by any instruments. There are large-scale choral festivals and national choral competitions, which are audible feasts of wonderful rich voices. Choir masters play a very important role, and some are renowned for their composing skills. The African part of the national anthem, "*Nkosi Sikilel' iAfrika*," which means "God Bless Africa" in Xhosa, was originally written as a hymn.

AFRICAN TRADITIONAL RELIGION

Traditional African religion is based on fundamentals such as ancestor worship. Believers practice Ubuntu (oo-buun-too), which is exemplified by treating others kindly, showing concern for others, and working for the good of the community. Focus is on family and special events such as birthdays, initiation ceremonies, weddings, and funerals. Animals are sacrificed for special events and to honor the spirits of the ancestors. However, nearly 80 percent of blacks today are Christians, and this acts as an important bond for the highly diverse population of South Africa.

Just under one-quarter of the Christians in South Africa are members of African Christian churches, especially the Zionist Christian Church (ZCC), which joins elements of traditional African beliefs with Christian values. The ZCC, the largest church in the country, has its headquarters at Moria in the Limpopo province. The rituals include the use of faith healing and revelation through dreams, riverine baptism, ritual garments, and dietary laws such as not eating pork. The Shembe Church in KwaZulu-Natal is similar to the ZCC, as it holds Christian beliefs that are integrated into traditional Zulu rituals. The Shembe Church observes rituals that include the washing of feet, keeping of the Sabbath, baptism by immersion, and fasting. There are approximately one million members of the Shembe Church in South Africa.

The trance dance by the San bush people.

Black and white missionaries have played a vital role in establishing schools, hospitals, and churches. They have presented Christianity to millions and have proved invaluable in the spiritual support, health, and education of the black population. Missionaries were also among the strongest opponents of apartheid.

RELIGION OF THE SAN PEOPLE

The San people believe that there is a great God who is good and very powerful. They either pray to Him by themselves or through a healer who is known as a *shaman* (shah-MAN). The trance dance is one of the most important rituals in the San religion. The women form a circle, sit around a fire, and clap to the rhythm of the spiritual songs that they sing while the men dance. As they clap, sing, and dance it is believed that the spirit enters the shamans and they go into a trance, at which time they get special healing powers.

WESTERN RELIGIONS

The majority of South Africans are Christians, even though a good number of them believe in an adapted form of Christianity or do not actively practice it. Most whites practice the Christian faith, although there are also strong Jewish communities, especially in the cities.

THE CHRISTIANS One of the larger Christian groups across the country, in the towns, cities, and rural areas, is the Dutch Reformed Church (DRC). Christianity originated from the early Dutch settlers, grew, and developed to its current form with the Afrikaners in South Africa. Many followers of the DRC supported apartheid and did not welcome blacks into their church. Daniel Francois Malan, the South African prime minister who led the campaign for complete segregation of the races in South Africa, was a minister of the DRC. The social segregation of blacks, Coloreds, and whites led to the establishment of churches for each of these three groups. In the early 1980s the World Alliance of Reformed Churches expelled the DRC from its organization after declaring apartheid to be a heresy. The DRC of South Africa no longer supports apartheid and the church has expressed repentance for the sin of supporting apartheid. It is to be hoped that following the establishment of voting for all adult South Africans, regardless of race, there will be closer integration within the church.

The Anglican and Methodist churches are also well supported, often by the English-speaking people. The Roman Catholic and Presbyterian churches have smaller followings in South Africa. A number of charismatic churches became popular from the 1970s onward. The most popular is the Rhema Church, which has its headquarters in Johannesburg.

The historic Anglican church in Knysna in Western Cape.

CHRISTIAN CHURCHES

A vast majority of South Africans are Christians, and many different denominations are represented in South Africa today.

THE DUTCH REFORMED CHURCH *The roots of this church can be traced back to the white settlers from the Netherlands in the early 17th century. The Dutch Reformed Church (DRC) in Africa was set up in 1859 and established orphanages and institutions for the underprivileged and needy. The Dutch Reformed Mission Church in South Africa was started in 1881 by congregations separated from the DRC in Africa. They originally started a church exclusively for Coloreds and people of racially mixed parentage. In 1986 all church congregations were desegregated, and many white opponents of apartheid joined it.*

THE PENTECOSTAL CHURCHES *The first Pentecostal churches were established in 1908. The late 1980s saw a drastic increase in the number of worshipers, especially among the blacks. The Apostolic Faith Mission Church is the largest Pentecostal church in South Africa. It played a big part in the Pentecostal movement that has swept across the continent.*

THE ROMAN CATHOLIC CHURCH *The influence of the Roman Catholic Church in South Africa began to grow after 1838, when the first resident bishop Patrick Raymond Griffith arrived in Cape Town from Ireland. With the help of two priests, he started his missions at Grahamstown, Port Elizabeth, and Uitenhage. When Griffith died in 1862 the Roman Catholic Church had been accepted as part of South Africa's religious establishment.*

THE METHODIST CHURCH *British soldiers brought Methodism to South Africa in 1806. The mission was launched by Barnabas Shaw, who came to the Cape in 1816, and William Shaw, who accompanied the British settlers of 1820. A mission was established among the Khoi at Leleifontein, and a chain of stations was established between the Cape Colony and Natal. Six missionary districts of the Wesleyan Methodist church became an affiliated conference in 1883. Many prominent black leaders are Methodists. The Methodist Church runs children's and old-age homes.*

THE JEWS Judaism has about 75,000 followers in South Africa. About 80 percent of South African Jews are Orthodox and belong to the Orthodox synagogue, but most are not strictly observant. The rest are Reform Jews. The largest population of Jews in South Africa is in Johannesburg. Jews believe that there is only one God and that a divine kingdom will be established on Earth. Jews go to the synagogue on the Jewish Sabbath, which lasts from Friday evening to nightfall on Saturday.

Muslim men carry out their prayers at the Sea Point beach front before the end of Ramadan fast.

OTHER RELIGIONS

THE MUSLIMS Followers of Islam are called Muslims. Their holy book, the Koran, is believed to have been revealed by God, called Allah, to the Prophet Muhammad. The roots of the South African Muslim community were among the Cape Malays and some of the Indian immigrants. Today there is a much larger and more widespread following, with about 650,000 members. They are still predominantly in Cape Town but also in Durban and Johannesburg.

THE HINDUS Most Hindus retained their religion when they came from India to South Africa and have since contributed to the community of more than 550,000 Hindus in South Africa today. They worship many gods and goddesses—some say there are as many as 300 million Hindu deities. The most important gods include Brahma, Vishnu, and Siva.

SANGOMAS The priests of the indigenous groups serve as voices of great authority. They are said to have spiritual powers that help them remove curses, make predictions, and establish links with ancestral spirits.

Sangomas, more often called traditional healers, deal in all forms of metaphysical healing, psychic skills, divination, clairvoyance, telepathy, and soothsaying. They also provide herbal medicine such as the traditional medicine called muti (MOOti) that consists of seeds, dried leaves, flowers, roots, herbs, bark, and animal tissue. A good number of Africans use traditional healers and herbal medicine to treat illnesses of both a physical and spiritual nature. It is a very old culture passed down from one generation to another. Within South Africa the term *sangoma* is used to describe a holy man or a holy woman who is a skilled diviner and healer within the tradition of Ndebele and Zulu native people. It takes many years to learn this practice because a healer is expected to know a great deal about the plants and animals—where and how to collect the items needed to make up the medicine—as well as to understand spiritual matters. A *sangoma* is similar to a naturopath in the United States, but with a spiritual dimension.

Many Africans believe that certain illnesses or accidents are caused by mythical creatures such as the *impundulu* (im-POON-DOO-loo), a large, white bird that feeds on human blood, and the *tokoloshe* (TAWK-o-LAWSH), a hairy dwarf that plays pranks and creates mischief. Both are equally feared for the misfortune they are believed to cause in villages.

INTERNET LINKS

www.tkm.co.za/doc/zcc.html

This website contains detailed information on the origins and characteristics of the Zion Christian Church.

www.rhema.co.za/Default.aspx

This is the official website of the Rhema ministries, with many links and information on the church.

www.africashamanexperience.com/about-us-meet-the-shamans-sangomas

This website contains information about *sangomas*—African healers—with explanations on divining methods, rituals, and their communications with ancestors.

LANGUAGE

The interior of Skoobs Theatre of Books, a two-story concept bookstore containing an vast collection of books. The bookstore also has a coffee shop and Champagne Bar for readers to enjoy both their books and beverages.

SOUTH AFRICA HAS ONE of the most diverse populations in the world, but does not have one language that is spoken by a majority of the population. The 11 languages recognized by the South African government are English, Afrikaans, Ndebele, Sepedi, Xhosa, Venda, Tswana, Southern Sotho, Zulu, Swazi, and Tsonga.

Most South Africans can speak more than one of the 11 official languages of South Africa. English and Dutch were the first official languages, but Afrikaans replaced Dutch in 1961 when South Africa became a republic. The main language of the government is English, and for commerce the main languages are English and Afrikaans.

WELKOM
IN DIE
NOORD-KAAP

O A AMOGELWA
MO KAPA
BOKONE

WELCOME
TO THE
NORTHERN CAPE

WAMKELEKILE
KUMTLA
KAPA

A sign bearing the phrase "Welcome to the Northern Cape" in four languages, Afrikaans, Tswana, English, and Xhosa.

Official documents are written in English and Afrikaans, but attempts are being made to incorporate more African languages, especially in schools and the media. There are also a growing number of books, magazines, and other media that are being published in English, Afrikaans, and the nine other languages.

THE VARIOUS TONGUES

In South Africa each ethnic group has its own language. In general, Coloreds speak Afrikaans, but those living in Cape Town can usually speak English as well. Asians speak English as well as their own languages, such as Tamil, Gujarati, Hindi, Cantonese, and Hakka. When talking among themselves, blacks use their own languages, such as Xhosa, Zulu, and Tswana. Many blacks use English or Afrikaans to communicate with others. Some, especially those who work in the mines, have also learned Fanakalo, a mixture of English, Zulu, and Afrikaans, which is another way to communicate with those who do not speak their language.

In the past English and Afrikaans were compulsory in schools, but students are now taught in English and in whichever of the other 10 languages is predominant in their area. For instance students in the Western Cape learn English and Afrikaans while students in KwaZulu-Natal learn English and Zulu.

AFRIKAANS

Afrikaans is one of the country's official languages. It had its beginning in 1651, when the Dutch language was brought to the new colony by settlers. Within 150 years Dutch was supplanted as the spoken language by a simpler

A schoolboy looks through the books in a library. Almost 20,000 of South Africa's public schools are lacking libraries. Equal Education, a movement working for equality of education, started the "1 School, 1 Library, 1 Librarian" campaign in a bid to increase the provision of libraries, especially in less-developed areas.

Fanakalo is a pidgin language developed mainly in the mines, where the many different tongues spoken by black workers created the need for a common language. Based on the vocabularies of Zulu, Xhosa, English, and Afrikaans, it is a common language that facilitates communication among the South Africans. It is a simple language with a vocabulary of only about 2,000 words.

version called Afrikaans. The main part of the Afrikaans vocabulary was derived from Dutch, but Afrikaans includes words and phrases from various African languages as well as Khoi, Xhosa, San, Malay, Portuguese, English, French, and German.

Afrikaans is an extremely descriptive language, which has coined a rich variety of new names for plants, animals, and words dealing with farming, hunting, and life in the bush. The names tend to be quite imaginative. For example the name of the town called Riviersonderend (rah-FEE-er-SAWN-dehr-ENT), translated literally, means "river without end." "Good day" is *goeie dag* (GHWEE-a-DAAGH), and "good-bye" is *totsiens* (TAWT-seens), meaning "until next sight."

In written form Afrikaans was probably used first in 1795 in a satirical poem during the British occupation of the colony. Great South African poets such as Eugene Marais and C. Louis Leipoldt helped popularize the language with their well-known works.

ENGLISH

Although the history of the British in South Africa only dates back to 1795, the English language was influenced by indigenous South African languages long before that time. In colonial South Africa English explorers, naturalists, and scientists who visited the land borrowed many native words to label new things they encountered. These included words to describe flora and fauna, topographical features, and customs.

The first English account of travels into the African interior was the journal of Francis Masson in 1775.

Two men read their morning newspapers at a cafe in Cape Town. Most newspapers in the country are published in English or Afrikaans.

As the use of English language extended across the land, more and more words of diverse origin were added to the vocabulary. A number of English words used commonly in South Africa cannot be understood by English speakers outside South Africa. Examples are bottle store (meaning "liquor store"), *robot* ("traffic light"), *braai* ("barbecue/grill"), *bakkie* ("small truck"), *biltong* ("jerky"), and *spoor* ("animal tracks").

South African English has also borrowed many words from Afrikaans. *Lekker* (LACK-kir) is a common word that describes tasty food or a particularly fun experience.

Many South Africans regarded Afrikaans as the language of racism and oppression because apartheid was devised and implemented by Afrikaans-speaking governments. For years the black schools of South Africa preferred to use English as the medium of instruction. Yet despite these negative feelings, many blacks and Coloreds speak Afrikaans better than English.

XHOSA

Xhosa is easily recognizable by the tongue-clicking sounds incorporated into the language and is spoken by approximately 18 percent of South Africa's population, roughly 8 million people. Xhosa is one of the languages derived from the Khoisan language and the word Xhosa means "angry men." Most of the languages in South Africa that include tongue-clicking originate from the Khoisan. Xhosa is classed as a Bantu language, as is Zulu; so if people who speak the languages of these two classes spoke to each other they would understand each other.

ZULU

Zulu is the mother tongue of 24 percent of South Africans and is understood by approximately 50 percent of the population. Zulu belongs to the Nguni group and is one of the Bantu languages. Xhosa and Zulu are mutually understandable. Zulu was a purely oral language until missionaries from Europe arrived and started writing down interesting facts concerning the language using the Latin alphabet. In 1883 an edition of the Bible was produced, which was the first book written in the Zulu language. The first Zulu language paperback, titled *Insila Kashaka*, was written by John Dube.

INTERNET LINKS

www.sa-venues.com/sa_languages_and_culture.htm

This website provides information on the languages and cultures of South Africa, including links to webpages dedicated to each of the 11 main languages.

www.ethnologue.com/show_country.asp?name=ZA

This website contains a detailed listing and brief information on all the languages spoken in South Africa.

www.dac.gov.za/bills/sa_language_bill.pdf

This site has many links and statistics dedicated to the languages of South Africa, both official and nonofficial.

ARTS

Rock paintings depict the life of the now-extinct San people spanning over 4,000 years. The extraordinary paintings of animals and human beings can be viewed up close by visitors of the Drakensberg National Park.

10

I N THE LAST 30 YEARS of apartheid the social and political climate influenced the arts. Protest theater was one way township dwellers expressed their frustration with apartheid, and playwrights such as Athol Fugard (1932—) and Gibson Kente (1932—2004) gave international exposure to the suffering of the blacks.

Today South African theater offers a wide variety of genres, from traditional European to traditional African shows. Much of the best theater is a reflection of the changes in South Africa toward becoming a multicultural country. Theater can take the traditional form of a play, but is often more vibrant and includes music, dancing, and sometimes even audience participation.

MUSIC

The African people have a rich and ancient musical tradition. This is either sung or played on instruments such as drums, reed pipes, and xylophones. Black music is based on traditional African themes, but recently it has undergone fundamental changes due to Western musical influence.

Traveling minstrel shows began to visit South Africa in the mid-1800s singing spirituals of the American South and influencing many South African groups to form themselves into choirs that were very popular at that time. The tradition of minstrel singing joined with other forms

Some of the most ancient art in the world, rock art created by the ancestors of today's Bushman and San, is found in South Africa. Today the country's people produce a wide range of traditional arts and crafts, including beadwork, basketry, and ceramics. Music, dance, and theater are popular at venues ranging from Bushveld festivals and botanical gardens to state-of-the-art theater complexes.

Traditional women play instruments and dance as part of a presentation in a village in KwaZulu-Natal.

and had its first international hit in 1939 with "Mbube." This song by Solomon Linda and the Evening Birds was an adaptation of a traditional Zulu melody and is the basis of Pete Seeger's hit "Wimoweh" and the internationally renowned classic "The Lion Sleeps Tonight." This was also performed by Timon and Pumbaa, the characters in Disney's classic movie and Broadway hit *The Lion King*.

The voices of Ladysmith Black Mambazo have joined the intricate rhythms and harmonies of South African musical traditions to Christian gospel music. The group had its first recording contract in 1970 and since has made more than 50 recordings. In the mid-1980s Paul Simon incorporated Ladysmith Black Mambazo's rich tenor, alto, and bass harmonies into his *Graceland* album. *Graceland* won many awards including the Grammy Award for Best Album of the Year. In 1987 Black Mambazo released *Shaka Zulu*, which won a Grammy Award for Best Traditional Folk Album. Since then the group has received 15 Grammy nominations and three Grammy Award wins, including one in 2009.

The increasing urbanization of black South Africans in mining centers such as the Witwatersrand resulted in the large settlements and townships where the miners lived. New forms of music began to develop. Marabi (ma-RAH-be) was the name given to a South African keyboard style that was similar to American ragtime and blues. It used a few simple chords that were repeated in various patterns. One of the offshoots of the marabi sound was kwela (KWE-lah) that became prominent in the 1950s. The main instrument of the kwela was the pennywhistle that was cheap, portable, and could be played as a solo instrument or in an ensemble. Lemmy Mabaso was one of South Africa's most famous pennywhistle players. The Xhosa singer Miriam Makeba, trumpeter Hugh Masekela, and jazz pianist Abdullah Ibrahim have achieved international recognition. The Soweto String Quartet, a classical and jazz group that adds African rhythm to some of its music, has also become well known around the world.

There are a few classical orchestras in South Africa. Previously most classical musicians were white, but today there are more black players. A number of classical players and composers, such as Arnold van Wyk and Kevin Volans, have contributed to the international classical style.

A table filled with handicrafts, such as tribal masks and animals, which are sold to tourists.

VISUAL ARTS

ROCK ART Some of South Africa's greatest art treasures are prehistoric rock art, or petroglyphs, that show lively images of animals, hunting scenes, and rituals. Many of the petroglyphs are at least 2,000 years old. There are about 3,000 protected rock art sites in the country.

HANDICRAFTS There is a growing handicraft industry in South Africa, and the more contemporary work includes cars or animals made out of wire and beads or Coca-Cola cans.

MODERN ART In the last decades of the 20th, century more black artists became well known and began selling their works to galleries and collectors. Their works depicted the hardships and injustices as well as the vibrancy of township life. Recently artists such as J. H. Pierneef (1886–1957), Walter Battiss (1906–82), Gerard Sekoto (1913–93), Mmakgabo Helen Sebidi (1943–), Karel Nel (1955–), Helena Hugo (1975–), and Titus Thabiso Matiyane (1964–) have added their styles to the growing mix of internationally known South African art.

INDIGENOUS ART Art produced by the various indigenous groups is very distinct. The Ndebele of Limpopo province are renowned for their brightly colored beadwork, while the Zulus are known for their shields and weapons, which are intricately stitched and made using a combination of hides and feathers. Carved wooden sculptures and beautiful woven cloths are among the traditional African art forms. Age-old handicrafts such as pottery, woodwork, mat-making, basketwork, and beadwork are still popular.

TRADITIONAL ARCHITECTURE

The Zulu homes found in KwaZulu-Natal are easily recognized by their beehive shape. The floor of the home is made of anthill soil, mixed and beaten smooth by the women of the kraal. A mixture of cow dung and water is smeared on the floor to improve its durability. The homes, which are made of dried grass, have no windows and only one arched opening for a doorway. Goatskins and mats make up the furnishing.

The most striking traditional African architecture is that of the Ndebele in southern Limpopo and Gauteng provinces. Graphic designs and intricate patterns are painted in bright colors on the walls of their homes. Artist Esther Mahlangu (1935—) has put her distinctive, brightly colored Ndebele designs on houses, cars, and even airplanes.

The houses in Zulu villages are simple structures, often without electricity and running water.

LITERATURE

South Africa has a wide variety of excellent authors from across its rainbow culture. Many of them are internationally well known, such as Nadine Gordimer (1923—), who won the Nobel Prize in Literature in 1991, and J. M. Coetzee (1940—), who won the British Booker Prize in 1983 and 1999, and the Nobel Prize in Literature in 2003.

For many years Afrikaans was scorned as a written medium, but in 1925, when it was finally recognized as an official language, more than 10,000 books were published in it. To reach an international market, some Afrikaner authors write in English as well.

There are a number of excellent Afrikaner writers. André Brink (1935—), a former teacher of literature at Rhodes University, has written many novels, including *A Dry White Season*, which criticizes apartheid. In 2010 his book *A Fork in the Road* was shortlisted for the Sunday Times Fiction Prize.

Playwright Athol Fugard's (1932—) works have been performed internationally. His plays, particularly *Boesman and Lena* and *"Master Harold"*

In 2011 South Africa's Handspring Puppet Company won a special Tony Award for the life-size puppets used in the highly acclaimed West End and Broadway play *War Horse*.

Ah, but your land is beautiful. Cruel and beautiful. A man is destroyed for a small sin of the flesh. For it is not a small sin of the flesh but a great sin against the nation. When you know that you will never look any man or woman in the eyes again, when you know that you will never smile or laugh again, when you know you will never jest again, then it is better to die than to live.

—Ah, But Your Land Is Beautiful *(1981), Alan Paton (1903—88)*

I remember those who used to live in District Six, those who lived in Caledon Street and Clifton Hill and busy Hanover Street. There are those of us who still remember the ripe, warm days. Some of us still romanticize and regret when our eyes travel beyond the dead bricks and split tree stumps and wind tossed sand.

—Buckingham Palace, District Six *(1986), Richard Rive (1931—89), a famous Colored author*

(Coloreds were forcibly removed from the suburb of District Six in Cape Town.)

Attend my fable if your ears be clean
In fair Banana Land we lay our scene—
South Africa, renowned both far and wide
For politics and little else beside.
The garden colony they call our land
And surely for a garden it was planned,
What apter phrase with such a place could cope
Where vegetation has so fine a scope,
Where weeds in such variety are found
And all the rarest parasites abound,
Where pumpkins to professors are promoted
And turnips into parliament are voted.

—The Wayzgoose *(1928), Roy Campbell (1901—57)*

... and the Boys, have received praise from around the world. In 2011 Fugard received the Tony Award for lifetime achievement.

Several English-speaking South African authors have achieved worldwide fame. Alan Paton (1903—88), who wrote Cry, the Beloved Country, is still one of South Africa's most famous authors, and Wilbur Smith (1933—) has publicized African game parks with his novels set in the bush. Nadine Gordimer, who has written many novels, used Burger's Daughter and July's People to show, through the format of a novel, the evils of apartheid.

Some of the first African works were by South African writers such as Thomas Mofolo (1876—1948), Solomon Plaatje (1876—1932), and R. R. R. Dhlomo (1901—71). Ingqumbo Yeminyana (The Wrath of the Ancestors) (1940) was written in Xhosa by Archibald Campbell Jordan (1906—68). It depicts the modern black author's exploration of urban life.

Censorship played a significant role in South Africa during the apartheid years. Newspapers, radio stations, and publishing firms were all subject to government control. Under the new government and constitution the rights to freedom of expression and freedom of the press are well guarded. This means that there is no unreasonable censorship of the media, the literature, and the arts.

INTERNET LINKS

www.mambazo.com/profile.php

This is the official website of the group Ladysmith Black Mambazo.

www.miriammakeba.co.za/

This is Miriam Makeba's official website, which includes information on the ZM Makeba Trust.

www.art.co.za/

This website contains links to webpages dedicated to many South African artists, including portfolios of their work and information on exhibitions.

Locals walk around and shop at the underground Carlton Centre Shopping Mall, linked to Carlton Centre, the tallest building in Africa. Over 180 shops, restaurants and an ice-skating rink are available here.

11

T

HE CLIMATE OF SOUTH AFRICA is ideally suited to many forms of outdoor leisure activity, ranging from sports such as rugby and mountaineering to deep-sea fishing to game viewing in the many parks around the country. The warm climate also encourages picnics and barbecues.

South Africans enjoy cultural performances and the theater. Many of the performances are held outdoors as well.

A crowd of people watch a live band perform as a source of entertainment at the Victoria and Albert Waterfront Amphitheatre in Cape Town.

In a recent survey of the leisure activities of South Africans it was found that the most time was spent socializing with the family, followed by watching TV, DVDs, and videos. Music-related activities and socializing with friends were also highly rated activities. Computers and the Internet, followed by crafts, occupied the least amount of leisure time.

During the apartheid years, many sanctions imposed had prevented the country's athletes from participating in international competitions. That is now a thing of the past, and many South African athletes take part in international competitions such as the Olympic Games.

LEISURE AND RECREATION

In the past people of different races were not allowed to mix socially and were forced to live in separate areas. As a result the different races developed different leisure lifestyles. After apartheid was abolished, the races began to mix with one another and people could enjoy whatever leisure activity they chose.

Family and friends come together at an outdoor location to have a *braai*. National Braai Day was declared in 2005 to promote historical inheritance as well as the food eaten in the country.

Popular in the townships is the practice of popping into a *shebeen* (sha-BEEN). This is similar to a pub but often less formal; it may even be a room in someone's house. People buy a drink and socialize with their friends.

The church is another popular gathering place, with the choir playing an important social role. Black Christians often get together to form choirs that are very popular in the community. During public choral performances, whole communities will turn up to sing and dance.

For the middle classes leisure time revolves around the family. Weekends are often spent outdoors. Friends and family get together to enjoy a barbecue, called a *braai* (br-EYE), which comes from the Afrikaans word *braaivleis* (br-EYE-flais) meaning "grilled meat." Barbecues take place at home around the swimming pool or at a chosen picnic spot.

South Africans who are more affluent often belong to community organizations such as chess clubs, wildlife societies, and bridge groups. Some families do volunteer work with organizations such as the Rotary Club and the Lion's Club that are found in most cities. Such organizations are popular fund-raising and social clubs that help needy communities.

The church also plays a significant role for the affluent. Many have their own community-help societies that render excellent service to the society they live in.

Theater, cabaret, and other forms of live entertainment are popular with affluent South African audiences, and numerous jazz clubs and live music venues are found in the major cities.

In the wealthier neighborhoods teenagers and twentysomethings mix freely and easily across cultural lines, especially since they have been to school together. The younger ones tend to have parties in the family home, while the older ones go out to clubs, movies, and bars.

SPORTS

South Africans are crazy about sports, whether they are spectators or participants. Since the 1994 democratic elections and the lifting of the sports ban, South African athletes have been welcomed back into the international

Friends meet up at Mitchell's Waterfront Brewery for a chat while lapping up assorted brews of beer.

Dedicated soccer fans come to show their support for the home team in the 2010 World Cup, which was hosted in South Africa.

The 2009 movie *Invictus* was about the South African team in the 1995 Rugby World Cup.

sports world. Soccer, rugby, and cricket are the major international sports played, but almost every warm-weather sport is represented and played at some level.

South Africa has produced many sports stars. Some of the best known include golfers Bobby Locke (1917—87), Gary Player (1935—), Ernie Els (1969—), and Sally Little (1951—); tennis stars Cliff Drysdale (1941—), Wayne Ferreira (1971—), and Johan Kriek (1958—); and world lightweight boxing champion Brian Mitchell (1961—).

Soccer, or association football, is the black national sport. Thousands of black spectators support their favorite teams in local, national, and international competitions. Most townships have vacant lots or fields where children can kick a ball around. Millions of dollars have been spent to improve sporting facilities at black schools.

In 1992 South Africa sent a team to the Olympics for the first time in decades. Runner Elana Meyer won a silver medal in the women's 10,000 meters at Barcelona. In 1996 Josia Thugwane won an Olympic gold medal in the men's marathon, and in 2008 Khotso Mokoena won a silver medal in the men's long jump event. Athletics has a large following, and there are about 500 running clubs with memberships in the hundreds of thousands. Long-distance and marathon events are often dominated by blacks. Fun-runs are popular fund-raisers for charity, but more serious runners compete in the many road races and marathons around the country each month. The ultimate achievement is the Comrades Marathon, an ultra-distance, 56-mile (90.1-km) route between Durban and Pietermaritzburg.

In the past cricket was a mostly white and Indian summer sport. Now schoolchildren are taking up the game seriously and there are exceptional players of all races on the national team. Rugby, once played mainly by whites and Coloreds, is now also played by all.

Public and private swimming pools are open to all races. Except for a few months during winter, South Africans swim throughout the year.

The annual Cape Argus Pick n Pay Cycle Tour hosts an average of 30,000 cyclists from the African continent and around the world yearly. The Tour is 68.4 miles (110 km) long and winds through some of the most beautiful coastal and mountain scenery in and around Cape Town. Johannesburg also hosts a long-distance day race each year, the Momentum 94.7 Cycle Challenge.

Since the lifting of sanctions on the country, South Africa has been organizing teams to compete internationally in boxing, golf, hockey, basketball, tennis, swimming, cycling, tenpin bowling, lawn bowling, squash, badminton, gymnastics, and ice skating. A more moderate climate gives South Africans a longer training season than their European and American counterparts.

South Africa is home to some of the most interesting stadiums in the world. Opened in 2009, the Moses Mabhida Stadium was designed to be a flexible facility with a nominal capacity of 54,000 that can be expanded to hold 80,000 people.

VACATION SPOTS

During the summer holidays most vacationers head for the coast, where there are many beaches to choose from, beginning with the fishing beaches of the southwestern coast to Cape Town's beaches to the beaches along the Garden Route, which stretches almost to Port Elizabeth. Along the coastal areas visitors can see whales in Hermanus (HER-ma-NIS), the rare Knysna Loerie bird (*Tauraco corythaix*) in Knysna (NIZE-na), and ostrich show farms in Oudtshoorn (OATS-HOERN).

The Gold Reef City Theme Park is a popular tourist destination, featuring an abundance of rides suitable for different people, from young children to adrenaline junkies.

In Cape Town visitors can experience the culture of the Cape Malays, who speak Afrikaans instead of their native Malay, but continue to make their superb spicy food. Visitors to the city flock to restaurants for seafood, especially the famed Cape lobsters. Eating is a serious business there. The Victoria and Alfred Waterfront development on Cape Town's harbor has restaurants, bars, and shops that never fail to attract large foreign crowds, as does the vibrant downtown area, which has many restaurants, pubs, theaters, and music clubs.

Durban's tropical climate draws many visitors to its beaches. International surfing competitions have been held at Durban's North Beach, and the famed Golden Mile is a concrete pavilion running the length of the seafront with water parks and amusements.

Vacationers can also visit Gold Reef City, a replica of Johannesburg during the gold rush days. It has modern entertainment facilities that include roller coasters, carousels, and shows featuring indigenous dancers. One favorite attraction is a cage that descends 720 feet (220 m) down a gold mine shaft.

Another favorite activity is taking the luxury Blue Train from Pretoria to Cape Town. The train is South Africa's version of the Orient Express and

The Blue Train seen at Matjiesfontein, a historic town in the Karoo.

is a hotel on wheels that takes passengers on a 1,000-mile (1,609-km) trip through some of the most scenic landscapes in the country. The train provides first-class meals served with silver on linen tablecloths.

Two hours' drive from Johannesburg is the famous Sun City complex. It has hotels, including the well-known exotic Palace of the Lost City, casinos, and an entertainment resort that has hosted shows by international rock stars. It is the largest man-made tropical paradise in the region.

THE GREAT OUTDOORS

Game and nature reserves and conservation areas abound in South Africa. Founded in 1898 the largest and most famous is the Kruger National Park in Mpumalanga province. It has about 150 species of mammals, more than 500 bird species, and many reptiles, amphibians, and fish. The Addo Elephant National Park is home to more than 550 elephants. Both black and white rhinoceroses can be seen at the Imfolozi Game Reserve. The various game reserves offer different kinds of accommodation, from simple village homes to luxurious bungalows. Two of the more luxurious game reserves, located within Kruger National Park, are Mala Mala and Sabi Sabi, where visitors are taken on guided game-spotting drives and served five-star meals outdoors.

Camping is also very popular with South Africans. There are hundreds of well-run campsites at the nature reserves, beaches, and game parks.

TELEVISION

Television was introduced in South Africa in 1975 and the first nationwide broadcast took place in January 1976. For years it was controlled by the state-owned South African Broadcasting Corporation (SABC), and programs and pro-apartheid news broadcasts alternated equally between English and Afrikaans. Today the SABC is an independent business. The SABC's broadcasting monopoly ended in 1986 when the subscription-based MNet was launched. Since 1994 a number of new television channels have been introduced by both the SABC and other private operators. Both the SABC and MNet broadcast across Africa. The SABC is a semipublic broadcaster and receives funding through advertising and license fees. It broadcasts on three domestic channels. South African television is broadcast in all 11 official languages as well as in German, Hindi, Portuguese, and even in sign. Although South Africa was one of the last in Africa to have a television service, there are now wide ranges of drama, comedy, sports, and news available on the channels.

MOVIES

South Africa's film industry has not been properly developed, but the country is gaining international appeal as a good location for making films. The country has a diverse natural landscape that provides many suitable locations for shooting movies. International filmmakers have found that it is less expensive to film in South Africa than in places such as Australia and Europe.

Gavin Hood's drama *Tsotsi* about a gangster in Soweto won the Academy Award for Best Foreign Language Film in 2006. The award followed an Oscar nomination for *Yesterday*, the story of the difficulties encountered by an HIV-positive mother, and *U Carmen E Khayalitsha*, a Xhosa-language film that won the Golden Bear Award at the 2005 Berlin Film Festival.

The majority of films on the circuit are American, although European films and art-house films are also shown in a fair number of movie theaters in the major cities. Movies are a major form of entertainment for many South Africans, and there are good-quality theaters in all the major towns and cities. The most popular venue for cinemas is inside massive shopping centers, where smaller theaters allow for five or ten movies to be screened at the same time.

INTERNET LINKS

www.saccd.org.za/objects/sabdc_reading.pdf

This site has a link to a survey into the reading and book reading behavior of adult South Africans, researched by the South African Book Development Council.

www.comrades.com/

This is the official website of the Comrades Marathon, with detailed information on this annual ultra-marathon.

www.cycletour.co.za

This is the official website of the cycle tour, with information on the history of the event, past tours, and how to enter future tours.

FESTIVALS

Locals wear colorful costume as part of the celebrations in the Minstrel Parade in Cape Town.

12

S OUTH AFRICA HAS A wide array of cultural and religious festivals. Since 1994 many public holidays, such as Republic Day, have been canceled, as they celebrated achievements during the apartheid days and were only relevant to whites.

New public holidays have been introduced that are celebrated by all South Africans. South Africans take great pride in their festivals and are very enthusiastic about these special days.

A band performs for a large audience at an outdoor concert during the Ebubeleni Arts Festival.

Festivals in South Africa take place throughout the year and are occasions where people can come together to celebrate anything from live music and the arts during the National Arts Festival or the Cape Town International Jazz Festival to whales at the Hermanus Whales Festival and even cherries at the Ficksburg Cherry Festival. South Africa has 12 annual public holidays. If a holiday falls on a Sunday, the Monday following it is declared a holiday.

A painting of the Battle of Blood River between the Voortrekkers and Zulus.

RECONCILIATION DAY

Reconciliation Day has been celebrated as a public holiday annually on December 16 since 1995. It was once called Dingaan's Day and, later, the Day of the Vow. The story of its origin lies in the history of the Great Trek.

The Afrikaners set out to explore the interior of South Africa during their Great Trek. When they arrived in KwaZulu-Natal, the stronghold of the Zulu kingdom, they reached an agreement with the great Zulu king Dingaan to secure large parts of the province. Dingaan misunderstood the intentions of the Afrikaners, and although he signed an agreement with their leader Piet Retief, he then ordered them to be killed. The Boers had left their weapons outside the camp and approximately 100 of their people were slaughtered on February 6, 1838. On December 16 that year, a Boer force of 470, having the advantage of gunpowder, fought and defeated Dingaan's 10,000-strong Zulu army at the Battle of Blood River. The battle was so named because the water turned red due to the blood of the 3,000 Zulus killed that day. From then on December 16 was known as Dingaan's Day. In 1952 the National Party renamed Dingaan's Day as the Day of the Covenant, which was subsequently changed to the Day of the Vow in 1980. The vow referred to is one the Boers made with God that if He helped them against the superior numbers of the Zulus, they would honor the 16th of December every year.

In the new South Africa the Day of the Vow was changed to Reconciliation Day. Although the Zulus lost they remember that day in festivities, sometimes in reenactments of the events that had happened. In celebrating the

Reconciliation Day, South Africans remember those battles and others, and remind themselves to strive for peaceful reconciliation and national unity among all of the country's people.

ART FESTIVALS

There are many festivals celebrating the arts in South Africa.

NATIONAL ARTS FESTIVAL Organized by the Grahamstown Foundation, this important annual cultural event offers a choice of the very best of both indigenous and imported talent. Over two weeks in July more than 50,000 people come to the city of Grahamstown for a feast of arts, crafts, and entertainment. The festival presents more than 500 shows, from stand-up comics and folk music to opera, cabaret, drama, and jazz. There are also market stalls selling products ranging from tie-dyed T-shirts and woven rugs to handmade jewelry and beaded crafts.

High Street, the main street in Grahamstown, is packed with people during the National Arts Festival.

The uniqueness of the town itself contributes to the festival's enormous success. Money that is raised is donated to the art community, and every year several prizes are awarded in the areas of sculpture, opera, music, and ballet. But more importantly the National Arts Festival brings together people of all races and ethnicities in a spirit of celebration.

KLEIN KAROO NATIONAL ARTS FESTIVAL This festival is held during March and April each year in Oudtshoorn. It began in 1994 and promotes all forms of arts and crafts in Afrikaans, but especially the visual and performing arts. Music plays a large role, and the festival even attracts acts from other countries such as the Netherlands, which has a language similar to Afrikaans. The festival offers an excellent program of classical music and many choirs also perform. The aim of the festival is to take a fresh look at the language and culture of the new South Africa and shake off the negative

Participants of the Cape Town Minstrel Carnival, also known as *Kaapse Klopse*, play musical instruments while walking in the parade.

Xhosa dancers at the National Arts Festival.

image of the apartheid era. It is a very successful festival and attracts people from all sections of the South African population. It has shown how so many South Africans can put their past differences behind them and move forward through artistic expression.

NAGMAAL FESTIVAL In the earlier times it was often difficult for Christians to receive Holy Communion every week because people lived far away from church and transportation was slow. Nagmaal, which means "Holy Communion" in Afrikaans, is a festival unique to South Africa. In the days when travel was slow and farm settlements were far apart, Afrikaners stayed home to pray most Sundays, but once every three months, large numbers would travel to town for religious services and for social reasons.

Today families go to Nagmaal in the nearest town where they attend church, catch up with family and friends, and shop for arts and crafts. It is no longer the huge social gathering that it once was. Only a small number of Afrikaners celebrate this festival to commemorate the past.

NEW YEAR'S DAY

New Year's Day festivities in South Africa are no different from those in many other countries, except there is no snow, as it is the middle of summer in the Southern Hemisphere. Celebrations take place outdoors, with picnics, barbecues, and swimming.

Every January Cape Town's biggest and most boisterous carnival, the Cape Town Minstrel Carnival, is celebrated. Festivities start on New Year's Day and continue well into January. Thousands of Colored minstrels with their painted faces and wearing brightly colored costumes and hats stroll through the streets playing their banjos and singing. It is a joyful and fun-filled festival. Like the performers in New Orleans' Mardi Gras, the minstrels are grouped in clubs, each with its own unique uniform. The clubs compete for annual prizes.

Some participants call this the Coon Carnival. The word *coon* does have a negative racial meaning, but some South Africans believe that it is part of their cultural history and so prefer to keep the original term. Others feel it is a racist word and call it the Minstrel Carnival.

A crowd of people sit on deck chairs or on the grass for an annual Christmas concert, *Carols by Candlelight*, on the lawns of Vergelegen Wine Estate, Somerset West.

CHRISTMAS AND EASTER

Christmas and Easter are public holidays in South Africa. Although not all South Africans take note of the religious significance of these days, they are happy to have a day off work.

Christmas celebrations are similar to those in other countries. The only exception lies in the fact that in South Africa it falls in summer. As such many South Africans opt for a barbecue outside instead of a traditional indoor meal. Some families attend church, and people spend what they can on special foods, a Christmas tree, and gifts for family and friends.

Easter is celebrated with public holidays on Good Friday and Family Day, which is the following Monday. Some businesses close on the Saturday as well, so many people take a long weekend off. Chocolate Easter eggs are usually hidden for children to find, and hot-cross buns are eaten on Easter Sunday. Most Christians attend church on Easter Sunday.

A memorial for Hector Peterson as well as other children, who was only 13 years old when he lost his life during the uprising against apartheid. Hector became an iconic image of the fateful day when a photograph of him being carried as he was dying was published all over the world.

OTHER HOLIDAYS

Aside from religious holidays such as Christmas and Easter, South Africa has a number of other holidays that mark certain milestones in the country's history.

HUMAN RIGHTS DAY On March 21, 1960, police killed 69 unarmed blacks in Sharpeville near Johannesburg as they took part in a protest demonstration against the oppressive laws of the government at the time. It was seen as a turning point in the fight for freedom from the human rights abuses of apartheid. Today March 21 is celebrated to remember every South African's human rights and to ensure they are never abused again.

The Roodepoort International Eisteddfod of South Africa (RIESA) was created in 1980 by an English expatriate, the late Keith Henry Fleming. First held in October 1981, a further eight events were staged every other year with the ninth and final event taking place in 1997, when financial support from the Roodepoort City Council ended.

RIESA was unique in that it invited only amateur soloists and groups who played to a very high standard to participate. Held every two years in October, it was the largest international music competition in the Southern Hemisphere. About 8,000 people from more than 60 countries competed in this gala event. Musical entries included categories such as classical soloists, choirs, instrumental, folk songs, folk dance, bands, orchestras, and original compositions.

RIESA was a nonprofit organization that organized the annual Eisteddfod in Roodepoort. When it deregistered it handed over a check to the Southern African Music Rights Organization (SAMRO) Endowment for the National Arts (SENA) for the establishment of an undergraduate bursary for music performance studies. A minimum of two bursaries per year for study in music performance are granted in the traditional (folk), jazz and Western art music genres. If there are no suitable candidates in a particular year, the bursaries are carried over to the following year.

FREEDOM DAY On April 27, 1994, South Africans voted for the first time in the country's history. It was the beginning of democracy for the country. Freedom Day is an annual celebration of South Africa's first nonracial democratic election.

YOUTH DAY June 16, 1976 was the beginning of the Soweto riots, when the anger of the township youth and, later, others around the country exploded against the oppressive segregated education and against the injustice of apartheid. June 16 is an official holiday that honors all the Soweto schoolchildren and youths who lost their lives in the fight for freedom.

NATIONAL WOMEN'S DAY In 1956 more than 20,000 women marched to the government buildings in Pretoria to protest against blacks having to carry identity documents and against the unfair apartheid laws. Today August 9 celebrates the contribution women make to the country and reminds everyone of the difficulties and prejudices many women still face today.

HERITAGE DAY South Africa is made up of many different cultures, languages, and traditions. On September 24 the country celebrates the good that comes from respecting cultural differences and enjoying the cultural wealth they bring to what Nelson Mandela called the Rainbow Nation.

INTERNET LINKS

www.grahamstown.co.za/index.php?pid=36

This website contains information on the annual National Arts Festival.

www.south-africa-tours-and-travel.com/index.html

This site has links to photographs and detailed information on the festivals of South Africa.

www.southafrica.info/about/history/sharpeville.htm

This website provides information on the origins of Human Rights Day and the events that took place on March 21, 1960.

www.info.gov.za/aboutsa/holidays.htm

This site contains listings of the dates of all official annual holidays, with links to information about the events that are being commemorated.

FOOD

A variety of ingredients in a typical African diet, from biltong, a dried and salted meat, to bread and spices.

13

SOUTH AFRICA'S FOOD IS AS RICH and varied as its people, combining the finest cuisines of Africa, Europe, and Asia.

GENERAL FOOD PRACTICES

South Africa grows an enormous variety of fresh fruits and vegetables. Locally produced beef, mutton, pork, chicken, and seafood are also available for the large variety of traditional dishes. Fast food and takeout have influenced people across the cultures, especially those in the towns and cities.

Fruits and vegetables on sale at a market. The province of Limpopo is the main farming location for the food.

South African food is a celebration of the country's rich cultural heritage and takes advantage of the wide variety of seafood, meat, game, and vegetables that are readily available. Some of the foods, such as crocodile sirloin steaks, fried caterpillars, and sheep heads, may be considered a culinary challenge by visitors, but more familiar items, such as hamburgers, sushi, and curry, are also available.

Different kinds of meat and vegetables on the barbecue during *braai*.

The Cape Malays and the Indians still use a wide variety of Eastern spices, while the Afrikaners favor a diet rich in meat and starch. Most city dwellers have adopted a general Western-style cuisine, with each immigrant group—Portuguese, Italian, Chinese, and African—adding some of its own traditional cooking concepts and ideas. Poorer communities in the townships and rural areas eat more cornmeal dishes because these are traditional and less expensive. The Italians, the Portuguese, the Chinese, the French, and the Greeks have kept to traditional cooking methods, and stores stock many foods and spices essential for these cuisines.

TRADITIONAL RURAL AFRICAN CUISINE

Traditional African food consumed mostly in the rural villages is simple and quite easy to prepare. Usually it is eaten out of a bowl, using the hands. Children are expected to wait until the adults have finished their meal.

Ground corn cooked with water into a smooth porridge called *pap* (PUP) is the staple food of many South Africans. Grinding the corn was traditionally a woman's job, but today it is often bought ready-ground. Herbs and spices are often added to the pap, which is rolled into balls and dipped in sauce made from green vegetables and chilies, or eaten with stewed meat. Meat is often used to denote status among members of each indigenous group. Men are usually given the head of the animal, which is regarded as the best part.

AFRIKANER CUISINE

The traditional Afrikaner meal includes one or more types of meat, potatoes, rice, and boiled vegetables often sweetened with sugar. This style of cooking originated on the farms, where meat was plentiful.

Today South Africans invite friends and family to enjoy a meal of salads, steak, chops, and spicy *boerewors* (BOO-rah-WAWRS), meaning "farmers' sausages" in Afrikaans, cooked over an outdoor fire. This form of entertaining has spread across the city and town suburbs.

Beef, ostrich, or kudu meat—cut into strips, salted, spiced, and dried in the sun— are an Afrikaans invention that many South Africans love. It is called *biltong*, the equivalent of beef jerky. It is an old Afrikaner staple from the time when it was necessary to have nourishing food that would not spoil during long treks into the country.

A *potjiekos*, or dutch oven, is used in traditional South African *braai*, or barbeque in Durban.

Afrikaners have a history of making delicious tarts and baked desserts. Some favorites include *koeksisters* (COOK-sis-ters), strips of plaited dough fried and soaked in syrup, and *asynpoeding* (uh-SAIN-PUH-duhng), vinegar pudding. Another popular treat, often eaten as breakfast, is the *beskuit* (buh-SKATE), or *rusk*, which resembles a chunk of dried bread and is usually eaten dipped in coffee or tea.

OTHER FOOD

The oldest and most typical fare on white South African tables combines the recipes the colonists brought from Europe with the richly spiced and curried dishes of the Cape Malays. *Bobotie* (bu-BOOH-tee), a curried meatloaf topped with milky egg; *sosatie* (sos-AA-ty), which is a kebab, usually of lamb meat

MELKTERT

14 ounces (400 grams) flaky puff pastry

1 egg white

4 cups (1 L) milk

1 cinnamon stick

4 tablespoons (60 ml) sugar

4 tablespoons (60 ml) all-purpose flour

Pinch of salt

2 tablespoons (30 ml) butter

4 medium eggs, beaten lightly

Ground cinnamon mixed with sugar

Line an 8-inch (20-cm) pie dish with a thin layer of the puff pastry, and brush lightly with the egg white. Heat the milk and cinnamon stick to just boiling. Mix the sugar, sifted flour, and salt in a bowl, and add the hot milk while stirring. Return the mixture to the pot, and heat at a low temperature (about 15 minutes) until it is thick. Remove from the heat, take out the cinnamon stick, and add the butter. Let the mixture cool, then add the beaten eggs, blending well with a spoon. Pour the mixture into the pastry shell, and bake at 450°F (230°C) for 15 minutes, then reduce the temperature to 325°F (165°C) for 15 minutes. Sprinkle with the cinnamon and sugar, and serve.

and sometimes fish, skewered and grilled; and *blatjang* (BLUT-yung), a tangy chutney made from fruit and used as a condiment instead of ketchup, are local adaptations of foods from both East and West.

As a refreshment many drink a local tea called *rooibos* (RAW-i-BAWS), which is made from the dried leaves and twigs of a scrubby bush. The rooibos (*Aspalathus linearis*) is a member of the legume family of plants. It contains no caffeine or tannin, and is also used in baking and fruit punches. It is an antioxidant and is believed to have health-giving properties.

RESTAURANTS

Competition among South Africa's restaurants is very stiff, and a restaurant cannot survive without maintaining high standards.

With such a mix of cultures, eating out is never dull as restaurants cater to all tastes. A wide range of cuisines—international, fusion, Italian, Portuguese, Chinese, Indian, Malay, and African—are available in many restaurants in all the major cities.

Some of the country's best seafood can be found along the Natal and Cape coast. Steak houses are popular with locals and are generally inexpensive. South Africans of Italian origin have opened many fine restaurants that are famous for their pasta. The Cape Malays' sweet curried dishes and Durban's hot Indian curries can also be sampled in a variety of restaurants in these areas.

Eating out is one form of entertainment that many wealthier South Africans enjoy, especially those living in cities and towns. With so many choices and a new urban culture that entertains regularly in restaurants, city dwellers dine out a few times a week. That and the increasing number of tourists encourage the range of South African restaurants to grow.

Locals having lunch at a restaurant in Stanford town centre in the Western Cape.

INTERNET LINKS

www.rainbowcooking.co.nz/

This website contains typical and traditional South African recipes.

www.southafrica.info/travel/food/

This website has food-related articles and information on South African cuisine.

www.uktv.co.uk/goodfood/homepage/sid/566

This website contains a link to a section on recipes, including South African specialties.

BOBOTIE (SPICE-BAKED MINCED MEAT)

This is a popular main dish among South Africans. It originated from mixing exotic spices brought by Malay slaves in the mid-1600s with Cape province ingredients, such as mutton and other game meat. Bobotie (bu-BOOH-tee) is often served with yellow rice.

1 thick slice of white bread

1 cup (250 ml) milk

Cooking oil

1 clove finely chopped garlic

2 roughly chopped onions

1 tablespoon (15 ml) curry powder

1 finely chopped chili pepper (optional)

2 pounds (900 g) ground lamb or venison

½ cup (125 ml) vinegar

1 tablespoon (15 ml) lemon juice

1 teaspoon (5 ml) brown sugar

1 tablespoon (15 ml) chutney

Preheat the oven to 320°F (160°C). Soak the bread, crust removed, in ½ cup milk, then squeeze the bread dry. Set aside. Heat the oil in a frying pan. Cook the garlic, onion, and curry powder (and chili if you are using it) over low to medium heat for 2 to 3 minutes. Add the meat, and fry until almost done. Add the bread, vinegar, lemon juice, brown sugar, and chutney, and cook for a minute. Remove from heat. In a pie dish that is 3 or 4 inches deep, place the bay leaves, two orange slices, and two lemon slices on the bottom. Fill the dish with the meat mixture. Beat the eggs and ½ cup milk, and pour over the meat. Bake uncovered for 30 minutes until the egg and milk form a custard on the top of the meat. To make the rice, bring the water, cinnamon, turmeric or saffron, and salt to a boil in a saucepan. Then add the rice and stir. Cook for 20 minutes over medium-to-high heat before adding the sugar and raisins. Simmer for another 20 minutes, then add the butter and stir well.

KLAPPERTERT (COCONUT TART)

This coconut tart is a popular dessert among South Africans.

1½ cups (375 ml) water

1½ cups (375 ml) sugar

3 cups (750 ml) finely grated fresh or desiccated coconut

6 tablespoons (90 ml) unsalted butter, cut into small bits

2 eggs and an additional egg yolk, lightly beaten

Splash of vanilla extract

2 tablespoons (30 ml) smooth apricot jam

1 baked short-crust pastry pie shell

8 strips candied citrus peel, one-inch long and ⅛-inch wide

Whipped cream (optional)

Preheat the oven to 350°F (175°C). Mix the sugar and water in a saucepan, and bring to a boil over high heat, stirring until the sugar dissolves. Boil the mixture until you can take some out and almost make a soft little ball. Do not stir while it is boiling. Take the pan off the heat,

add the coconut and butter, and stir until the butter has melted. Let the mixture cool to room temperature, then mix the egg and vanilla, and vigorously beat into the mixture. Melt the apricot jam over very low heat, stirring constantly, then brush it evenly over the bottom of the baked pie shell. Pour the coconut mixture into the pie shell, spreading it smoothly. Bake for about 40 minutes. Filling should be firm and golden brown. Before serving, arrange the thin strips of candied peel in a pattern on the pie top. Serve it at room temperature, with whipped cream if you choose.

A   **B**   **C**   **D**

ZIMBABWE

1

Tropic of Capricorn

BOTSWANA

Messina   *Limpopo*

MOZAMBIQUE

Limpopo River Valley

LIMPOPO

Pietersburg

Kruger

National

Park

NAMIBIA

K a l a h a r i

D e s e r t

Sun City   **GAUTENG**

PRETORIA

Mafikeng *Witwatersrand*

Soweto Johannesburg

Germiston Springs

Vereeniging

MPUMALANGA

SWAZILAND

NORTH WEST

Piet Retief

2

Kuruman

Vaal

Odendaalsrus

Welkom Virginia

ZULULAND

KWAZULU-

NATAL

Alexander

Bay *Namaqualand*

Orange

Kimberley

FREE STATE

Bloemfontein

LESOTHO

▲ Champagne Castle

(11,073 ft / 3,374 m)

Pietermaritzburg

Durban

3

NORTHERN CAPE

Prieska

Orange

De Aar

Aliwal

North

Drakensberg Mountains

Kokstad

Port Edward

ATLANTIC OCEAN

Calvinia

Umtata

Beaufort West

Great Karoo

EASTERN CAPE

East London

Grahamstown

Port Alfred

WESTERN CAPE

Langeberg Mts.

Little Karoo   Oudtshoorn

Uitenhage

Table Mt. ▲ Stellenbosch

Cape Town

Plettenberg

Bay

Port Elizabeth

N

↑

4

Cape of

Good Hope

Cape Agulhas

INDIAN OCEAN

5

	Capital city
●	Capital city
•	Major town
▲	Mountain peak

Feet		Meters
16,500		5,000
9,900		3,000
6,600		2,000
3,300		1,000
1,650		500
660		200
0		0

MAP OF SOUTH AFRICA

Alexander Bay, A3
Aliwal North, C3
Atlantic Ocean,
  A3—A5

Beaufort West, B3
Bloemfontein, C3
Botswana, B1—B2,
  C1—C2

Calvinia, A3
Cape Agulhas, A4
Cape of Good Hope,
  A4
Cape Town, A4
Champagne Castle,
  D3

De Aar, B3
Drakensberg
  Mountains, C3,
  D3
Durban, D3

Eastern Cape,
  B3—B4, C3—C4
East London, C4

Free State, C2—C3,
  D2

Gauteng, C2
Germiston, C2
Grahamstown, C4
Great Karoo, B4

Indian Ocean,
  B4—B5, C4—C5,
  D2—D5

Johannesburg, C2

Kalahari Desert,
  A2, B2
Kimberley, C3
Kokstad, D3
Kruger National
  Park, D1, D2
Kuruman, B2
KwaZulu-Natal, D2,
  D3

Langeberg
  Mountains, A4,
  B4
Lesotho, C3
Limpopo, C1—C2,
  D1—D2
Limpopo River, C1,
  D1
Limpopo River
  Valley, C1
Little Karoo, B4

Mafikeng, C2
Messina, D1
Mozambique, D1—
  D2
Mpumalanga, D2

Namaqualand, A3
Namibia, A1—A2
Northern Cape,
  A2—A3, B2—B3,
  C2—C3
North-West, B2, C2

Odendaalsrus, C2
Orange River, B3,
  C3
Oudtshoorn, B4

Pietermaritzburg,
  D3
Pietersburg, D1
Piet Retief, D2
Plettenberg Bay,
  B4
Port Alfred, C4
Port Edward, D3
Port Elizabeth, C4
Pretoria, C2
Prieska, B3

Soweto, C2
Springs, C2
Stellenbosch, A4
Sun City, C2
Swaziland, D2

Table Mountain, A4

Uitenhage, C4
Umtata, C3

Vaal River, C3
Vereeniging, C2
Virginia, C2

Welkom, C2
Western Cape,
  A3—A4, B3—B4
Witwatersrand, C2

Zimbabwe, C1, D1
Zululand, D2

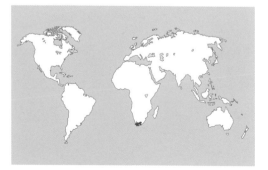

ECONOMIC SOUTH AFRICA

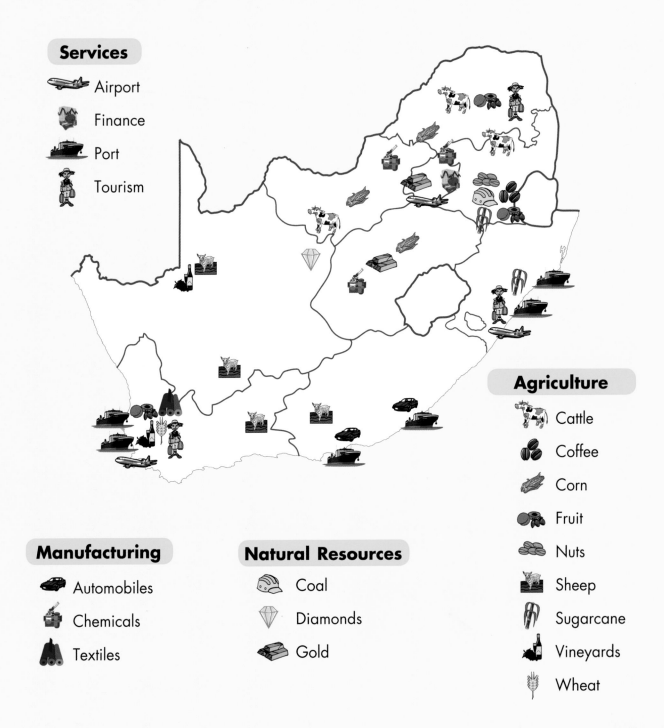

Services
- ✈ Airport
- Finance
- Port
- Tourism

Agriculture
- Cattle
- Coffee
- Corn
- Fruit
- Nuts
- Sheep
- Sugarcane
- Vineyards
- Wheat

Manufacturing
- Automobiles
- Chemicals
- Textiles

Natural Resources
- Coal
- Diamonds
- Gold

ABOUT THE ECONOMY

OVERVIEW

In 1994 the newly elected government set strict, sound economic principles to increase economic growth. The rate of inflation, once very high, decreased. Growth was vigorous from 2004 to 2007 as South Africa reaped the benefits of macroeconomic stability and a global commodities boom. In the second half of 2007 growth slowed due the global financial crisis's impact on commodity prices and an electricity crisis. GDP fell nearly 2 percent in 2009 but recovered since then. Economic policy has focused on controlling inflation, but significant budget deficits has restricted the government's ability to deal with the pressing economic problems of unemployment, poverty, and income inequality.

GROSS DOMESTIC PRODUCT (GDP)

$592 billion
Per capita: $11,600 (2012 estimate)

INFLATION RATE

5.7 percent (2012 estimate)

CURRENCY

1 South African rand (ZAR) = 100 cents
USD 1 = ZAR 9.95 (October 2013)
Notes: 10, 20, 50, 100, 200 rand
Coins: 1, 2, 5, 10, 50 cents

GDP SECTORS

Agriculture 2.6 percent, industry 29.3 percent, services 68.1 percent (2012 estimate)

WORKFORCE

18.06 million (2012 estimate)

LABOR DISTRIBUTION

Agriculture 9 percent, industry 26 percent, services 65 percent (2012 estimate)

UNEMPLOYMENT RATE

22.7 percent (2012 estimate)

AGRICULTURAL PRODUCTS

Beef, corn, dairy products, fruits, mutton, poultry, sugarcane, vegetables, wheat, wool

INDUSTRIAL PRODUCTS

Automobile assembly, chemicals, chromium, fertilizer, gold, iron, steel, metalworking, machinery, platinum, textiles, commercial ship repair

MAJOR TRADE PARTNERS

China, Germany, India, Japan, the United Kingdom, the United States

MAJOR EXPORTS

Coal, diamonds, fruit, gold, iron, manganese, platinum, steel, uranium, vegetables, machinery and equipment

MAJOR IMPORTS

Machinery and equipment, foodstuffs, chemicals, scientific instruments, petroleum products

CULTURAL SOUTH AFRICA

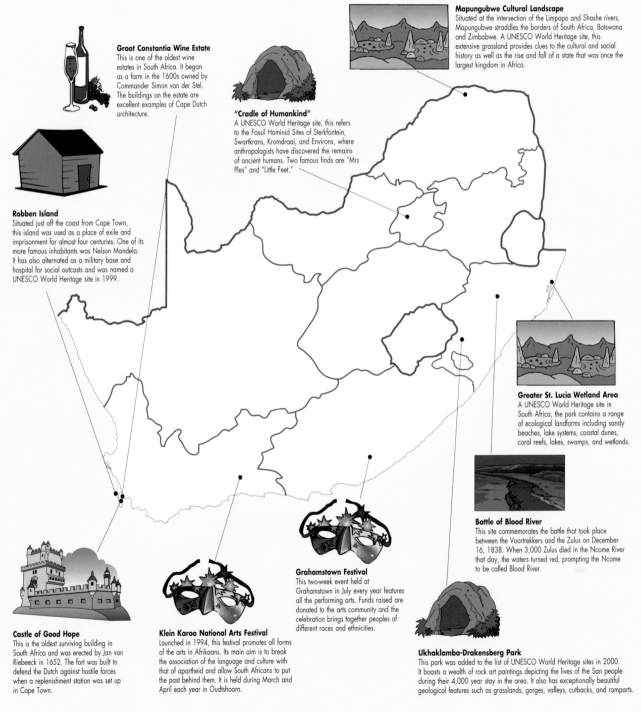

Groot Constantia Wine Estate
This is one of the oldest wine estates in South Africa. It began as a farm in the 1600s owned by Commander Simon van der Stel. The buildings on the estate are excellent examples of Cape Dutch architecture.

Mapungubwe Cultural Landscape
Situated at the intersection of the Limpopo and Shashe rivers, Mapungubwe straddles the borders of South Africa, Botswana and Zimbabwe. A UNESCO World Heritage site, this extensive grassland provides clues to the cultural and social history as well as the rise and fall of a state that was once the largest kingdom in Africa.

"Cradle of Humankind"
A UNESCO World Heritage site, this refers to the Fossil Hominid Sites of Sterkfontein, Swartkrans, Kromdraai, and Environs, where anthropologists have discovered the remains of ancient humans. Two famous finds are "Mrs Ples" and "Little Feet."

Robben Island
Situated just off the coast from Cape Town, this island was used as a place of exile and imprisonment for almost four centuries. One of its more famous inhabitants was Nelson Mandela. It has also alternated as a military base and hospital for social outcasts and was named a UNESCO World Heritage site in 1999.

Greater St. Lucia Wetland Area
A UNESCO World Heritage site in South Africa, the park contains a range of ecological landforms including sandy beaches, lake systems, coastal dunes, coral reefs, lakes, swamps, and wetlands.

Battle of Blood River
This site commemorates the battle that took place between the Voortrekkers and the Zulus on December 16, 1838. When 3,000 Zulus died in the Ncome River that day, the waters turned red, prompting the Ncome to be called Blood River.

Castle of Good Hope
This is the oldest surviving building in South Africa and was erected by Jan van Riebeeck in 1652. The fort was built to defend the Dutch against hostile forces when a replenishment station was set up in Cape Town.

Klein Karoo National Arts Festival
Launched in 1994, this festival promotes all forms of the arts in Afrikaans. Its main aim is to break the association of the language and culture with that of apartheid and allow South Africans to put the past behind them. It is held during March and April each year in Oudtshoorn.

Grahamstown Festival
This two-week event held at Grahamstown in July every year features all the performing arts. Funds raised are donated to the arts community and the celebration brings together peoples of different races and ethnicities.

Ukhaklamba-Drakensberg Park
This park was added to the list of UNESCO World Heritage sites in 2000. It boasts a wealth of rock art paintings depicting the lives of the San people during their 4,000 year stay in the area. It also has exceptionally beautiful geological features such as grasslands, gorges, valleys, cutbacks, and ramparts.

ABOUT THE CULTURE

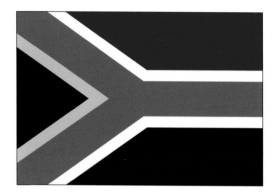

OFFICIAL NAME
Republic of South Africa

NATIONAL FLAG
The colors reflect the four major political parties and combines with a distinctly African character. The broad green stripes flowing into one symbolize the convergence of the past and future.

NATIONAL ANTHEM
National Anthem of South Africa, combining "The Call of South Africa" ("Die Stem van Suid-Afrika") and "Nkosi Sikelel iAfrika."

CAPITAL CITIES
Pretoria is the administrative capital, Cape Town is the legislative capital, and Bloemfontein is the judicial capital.

MAJOR CITIES
Durban, East London, Johannesburg, Pietermaritzsburg, Port Elizabeth

POPULATION
48.6 million (2013 estimate)

LIFE EXPECTANCY
49.48 years (2013 estimate)

ETHNIC GROUPS
Asians, blacks, Coloreds, whites

RELIGIONS
Christians, Roman Catholics, Muslims

MAJOR LANGUAGES
Afrikaans, English, Ndebele, Sepedi, Southern Sotho, Swati, Tsonga, Tswana, Venda, Xhosa, Zulu, others

ADMINISTRATIVE DIVISIONS
Eastern Cape, Free State, Gauteng, KwaZulu-Natal, Limpopo, Mpumalanga, Northern Cape, North-West, Western Cape

BIRTH RATE
19.14 births/1,000 population (2013 estimate)

DEATH RATE
17.36 deaths/1,000 population (2013 estimate)

INFANT MORTALITY RATE
42.15 deaths/1,000 live births (2013 estimate)

LITERACY RATE
93 percent of adults older than 15 years old can read and write (2011 estimate)

TIMELINE

IN SOUTH AFRICA	IN THE WORLD

circa 8000 B.C.
San peoples depict objects and events in rock painting in the Drakensberg region.

circa 1000–800 B.C.
Bantu peoples spread through sub-Saharan Africa.

A.D. 300
Early South African Iron Age farmers lay the foundations of South Africa's mining industry.

1206–1368
Genghis Khan unifies the Mongols and starts conquest of the world. At its height, the Mongol Empire under Kublai Khan stretches from China to Persia and parts of Europe and Russia.

1488
Portuguese sailor Bartholomeu Dias lands on South African soil.

1652
Jan van Riebeeck, representing the Dutch East India Company, sets up refreshment port at what is now Cape Town.

1688
French Huguenot refugees arrive and settle at the Cape.

1820
The British arrive.

1789–99
The French Revolution

1835
Boers leave Cape Colony and the Great Trek begins.

1838
Boers defeat the Zulus and set up the first republic in KwaZulu-Natal.

1867
Diamonds discovered at Kimberley.

1880
Boers rebel against the British sparking the first Anglo–Boer War.

1899
The second Anglo–Boer War starts.

1902
Treaty of Vereeniging ends the second Anglo-Boer War.

1910
The Union of South Africa is formed, with General Louis Botha as the first prime minister.

1912
Native National Congress founded, later renamed African National Congress (ANC).

1913
Land Act introduced to prevent blacks, except those living in Cape province, from buying land outside reserves.

1914
World War I begins.

IN SOUTH AFRICA	IN THE WORLD
1919 •	
Botha dies; Jan Christian Smuts takes over as prime minister.	• **1939** World War II begins.
1948 •	
Smuts is ousted by the National Party led by D. F. Malan, who introduces apartheid.	
1955 •	
Hendrik Verwoerd succeeds Malan and tightens apartheid policy.	
1960 •	
Sharpeville Massacre takes place. ANC is banned.	
1961 •	
White South Africa severs ties with the Commonwealth and becomes a republic.	
1964 •	
Iconic anti-apartheid leader, Nelson Mandela is sentenced to life imprisonment.	
1966 •	
Prime Minister Hendrik Verwoerd is assassinated.	
1990 •	
F. W. de Klerk declares apartheid dismantled.	
1994 •	
The first democratic elections are held; Nelson Mandela becomes president.	
1996 •	• **1997** Hong Kong is returned to China.
The constitution of South Africa is adopted. The Truth and Reconciliation Commission is established.	
1999 •	• **2003** War in Iraq begins.
The ANC wins the second democratic elections; Thabo Mbeki becomes president.	
2004 •	• **2004** Eleven Asian countries are hit by giant tsunami, killing at least 225,000 people.
ANC win landslide election. Thabo Mbeki begins his second term as president.	
2008 •	• **2008** Earthquake in Sichuan, China, kills 67,000 people.
President Mbeki resigns. ANC deputy leader Kgalema Motlanthe is chosen by Parliament as president.	
2009 •	• **2009** Outbreak of flu virus H1N1 around the world
Parliament elects Jacob Zuma as president.	
2010 •	
South Africa hosts the World Cup.	
2013 •	• **2013** The first African American US president, Barack Obama, begins his second term.
Nelson Mandela is in precarious health.	

GLOSSARY

Afrikaans
The language of the Afrikaners, closely related to Dutch and Flemish.

apartheid (a-PAHRT-hate)
A policy of racial segregation and discrimination in South Africa before F. W. de Klerk's presidency; originally it was an Afrikaans word meaning "separation."

Boer (BOO-er)
"Farmer" in Afrikaans.

boeremusiek (BOO-rah-moo-SIK)
Music played by an Afrikaans band.

braaivleis (br-EYE-flais)
Meat grilled over the fire.

fynbos (f-AY-n-BAWS)
A term that describes more than 25,000 plant species indigenous to South Africa.

Homelands
Tracts of land set aside by the apartheid government for non-whites to live on.

Khoisan (koi-SAN)
A nomadic indigenous group.

kraal
An indigenous settlement.

kwela (KWE-lah)
Funky jazz music that originated in the black townships.

Ndebele (ng-de-BEE-leh)
An African indigenous group.

pap (PUP)
A porridge made from ground corn.

rooibos (RAW-i-BWAS)
Local tea made from dried stalks of a scrubby bush that grows in the southeastern regions.

sangoma (sung-GAW-mah)
A medicine man.

segregation
The separation of people according to their ethnic group or race.

shebeen (sha-BEEN)
An illegal drinking house where homemade beer is brewed and served.

townships
Black settlements that sprang up on the outskirts of cities during the apartheid years when blacks and whites were forced to live separately.

veld
Open country with grassy patches.

Voortrekkers (FOO-ehr-trekkers)
The first group of Boers who ventured into the South African interior; from the Afrikaans word meaning "front trekkers."

Xhosa (KAW-sah)
One of the Nguni groups.

FOR FURTHER INFORMATION

BOOKS

Chimeloane, Rrekgetsi. *Whose Laetie Are You?* Roggebaai: Kwela Books, 2001.

Hilton-Barber, Brett and Lee R. Berger. *Official Field Guide to the Cradle of Humankind*. Cape Town: Struik Publishers, 2002.

Holland, Heidi and Adam Roberts (Eds.). *From Jo'burg to Jozi*. London: Penguin, 2011.

Lottering, Agnes. *Winnefred and Agnes: The True Story of Two Women*. Roggebaai: Kwela Books, 2002.

Malam, John. *The Release of Nelson Mandela (Dates with History)*. Weybridge, VT: Cherrytree Books, 2008.

Mandela, Nelson. *The Illustrated Long Walk to Freedom (Illustrated and abridged ed.)*. New York: Little Brown Company, 2006.

Paton, Alan. *Cry, the Beloved Country*. London: Vintage Classics, 2002.

WEBSITES

African National Congress. www.anc.org.za

Banknotes of South Africa. www.banknotes.com/za.htm

Central Intelligence Agency World Factbook (select South Africa from the country list). www.cia.gov/cia/publications/factbook

National Department of Agriculture (NDA).www.nda.agric.za

Nobel e-Museum: Nelson Mandela Biography. www.nobel.se/peace/laureates/1993/mandela-bio.html

Parliament of South Africa.www.parliament.gov.za

South Africa: Alive with Possibility (official Internet gateway). www.safrica.info

South African Government Department of Environmental Affairs and Tourism. www.environment.gov.za

South Africa Government Online. www.gov.za

South African Missions in New York. www.southafrica-newyork.net

South African National Parks (SANParks). www.parks-sa.co.za

The World Bank Group (type South Africa in the search box). www.worldbank.org

DVDS/FILMS

Cry Freedom. Universal Pictures UK, 2001.

Sarafina. Miramax Echo Bridge, 2011.

Tsotsi. Momentum Pictures Home Entertainment, 2006.

BIBLIOGRAPHY

BOOKS

Hughes, Libby. *Nelson Mandela: Voice of Freedom*. Bloomington: iUniverse, 2000.

Miesel, Jaqueline. *South Africa at the Crossroads*. Highland Park, NJ: Millbrook Press, 1994.

Pascoe, Elaine. *South Africa: Troubled Land*. New York: Franklin Watts, Inc., 1987.

Paton, Jonathan. *The Land and People of South Africa (Portraits of the Nations)*. Philadelphia: Lippincott Williams & Wilkins, 1990.

Smith, Chris. *Conflict in Southern Africa*. New York: New Discovery Books, 1993.

Thompson, Leonard M. *A History of South Africa*. New Haven, CT: Yale University Press, 1990.

Worden, Nigel, et al. *The Chains That Bind Us: A History of Slavery at the Cape*. Cape Town: Juta Gariep, 1996.

WEBSITES

Embassy of South Africa in The Hague, Netherlands. www.zuidafrika.nl/

South Africa Info: Arts and Culture. www.southafrica-newyork.net/consulate/arts.htm

South African Indian Collections. scnc.udw.ac.za/doc/Coll/SAINDCOL.htm

South African Albums: Vineyard Music. www.worship.co.za/pages/za.asp

South African Reserve Bank.www.reservebank.co.za

South Africa's National Holidays. http://africanhistory.about.com/library/bl/blsaholidays.htm

Truth and Reconciliation Commission. www.justice.gov.za/trc/index.html

INDEX

INDEX